Self-Publishing and Collection Development

Opportunities and Challenges for Libraries

Self-Publishing and Collection Development

Opportunities and Challenges for Libraries

Edited by Robert P. Holley

Charleston Insights in
Library, Archival, and Information Sciences

Purdue University Press
West Lafayette, Indiana

Contents

Foreword

Mitchell Davis, BiblioLabs

Katina Strauch, the founder of the Charleston Conference (and a leader of the editorial board of this series of books), has a fantastic vision and drive, as anyone who knows her will attest. The first time I met her, someone brought her to our offices (also located in Charleston) for a show-and-tell tour. As she wandered into BookSurge in 2003, I am sure she was uncertain what to make of the ragtag bunch trying to change the publishing industry.

Our offices were "uptown" behind a fried chicken restaurant dumpster and next to a bingo parlor that was held up at gunpoint as we conducted meetings in the front office one day. We found bullet casings in the parking lot all the time. Despite these bleak surroundings, she was nice to me, she was curious about the publishing and print-on-demand business we had built out of those humble beginnings, and she made me a part of her conference the following year. We became friends, and she continues to be an inspiration to me.

Several years later, she invited me to put together a plenary session on libraries and self-publishing for the Charleston Conference. At that point, I had sold BookSurge to Amazon.com, had moved to Seattle to integrate the company and technology, and had come a long way from those ragtag, strip mall, bingo parlor days. I worked at Amazon for two years after the sale, helping to turn BookSurge into CreateSpace, now the world's largest and most successful self-publishing company.

I suppose as an early self-publishing visionary—and because I was now a part of the library industry with our new company BiblioLabs—she thought I would be good to put together the plenary. It was a huge hit. It was one of those Charleston Conference sessions where people pour over into the hallways and ask questions remotely while watching on closed-circuit television in another room. We definitely felt like we were onto something.

The next year, she asked if I could do a preconference on the same topic. I jumped at the chance and was able to convince some of the best brains and the most entertaining people in the library and publishing world to come debate the topic for half a day. It was an inspiring day for everyone who attended and had a chemistry I have yet to see in a conference of its type.

This resulting book is the product of the conversation Charles Watkinson and I had afterward. At the time, Charles was the director of Purdue University Press, and he had delivered a fantastic presentation on what he was doing within the organization to facilitate self-publishing. We were still buzzing from the day's activity and discussing how the day had uncovered more honest ways to think about and talk about self-publishing in academia. I had called the preconference "Self Pub 2.0," attempting to convey the idea that self-publishing was a technology revolution entering a new phase—that at the end of the day technology could be applied in any way the imagination saw fit.

I still got resistance to the name of the preconference. The words "self-publishing" had a scarlet letter feel, the lingering effect of the vanity publishing era where printers dubiously sold truckloads of books to ambitious authors. My perspective on this was shaped early in my BookSurge career. In 2001, one of my partners at the time, Jeff Schwaner, calmly told a room of New York City publishers who were accusing self-publishing companies of being vanity publishers: "All publishing is vain, and that is OK."

I stuck to my guns on the name and knew I was right when Charles (one of the leaders of the "libraries as publishers" movement) said to me in our conversation afterward, "I realize now this is not library publishing, but *library-facilitated self-publishing*." I felt a bit of the scarlet leave the letter as he said it. I am very proud to have had that spark lead to this important book.

The articles you will find here are an excellent course in the thinking surrounding the marriage of self-publishing and libraries. I was happy to see the text depart from a strict academic context to create a mesh of perspectives that let all range of libraries learn from the experiences of others. Publics, academics, and community college libraries all are represented here.

Several themes strike me throughout the book, including 1) the power of self-publishing as a generator of primary source materials, 2) the effects of Amazon on the role of libraries, and 3) the changing business of publishing (in large part driven by the aforementioned retailing powerhouse).

Much credit for this book goes to Bob Holley, a fantastic editor and all-around book wrangler, as well as one of the top library thinkers on the issue of self-publishing. During the original "Self Pub 2.0" preconference, he gave us all an increased perspective on self-publishing as a generator of primary source materials. The coverage he gives that topic here is excellent. It reminded me of talking to the director of the Peace Corps Writers program in those early days of self-publishing, who told me, "You know half the people in the Peace Corps are writing a book . . . and most of them suck. But you know what? When the Ken Burns of the next generation comes along, and there is no longer a thing called the Peace Corps, it won't matter that they suck." Self-publishing provides—and will continue to provide—an unprecedented record of human history and experience. I am happy to see Bob so articulately cover this topic, as well as give several other strong arguments for why academic libraries should acquire self-published materials.

Several authors deal with the topic of Amazon from the author perspective, but Bob Nardini and Eleanor Cook point out the real challenges Amazon poses to the institution of the library as the world moves more indie. Nardini, after giving a landscape of library vendor options, correctly points out that Amazon (not any library vendor) is the database of record for self-published and indie books, because authors think about Amazon first and libraries later.

When I worked at Amazon integrating BookSurge, I once was asked to write a report on the potential for Amazon to get into the library business "properly" (i.e., MARC records, shelf-ready books, etc.). After writing the report (which did not take a position on whether it was a good or bad idea, just delivered facts), we met with a smart vice president to review the plan. He sat at his desk, read about two paragraphs, and then put the document down. He looked at us and said, "Do you realize we are probably the largest seller of books to libraries in the United States, and we have no one in the building thinking about libraries?" The meeting ended about two minutes later, and it never came up again.

He was right. Amazon, by simply making things easy to order and then delivering them faster and cheaper than other library vendors, had leapfrogged companies serving libraries for decades without even trying. Visit the receiving area of a library sometime and look at the logos on the boxes if you doubt this.

There is a lesson in this that libraries should take to heart. Cook points out in her piece that "avid readers of indie books often completely bypass the library for discovery since these books are often readily available free or at a nominal price."

At the risk of seeming histrionic, in many regards, the library's ability to survive as an institution depends on it being an effective and valuable part of this indie ecosystem. Amazon's attitude is that the "institution" of the library (as it is currently set up and managed) actually gets in the way of executing on the vision of a library. If every book, movie, and song is available in a simultaneous use model via Kindle Owners' Lending Library for a nominal price, who needs libraries?

As offensive as this may seem, there is no article that will be written, conference presentation delivered, or moral argument made to change this attitude, because they keep winning. The only answer for ensuring there is a prominent long-term digital role for the library is for libraries to successfully execute against a vision that is bigger, bolder, and more inclusive than Amazon's. This relies in large part on not remaining insulated and seeing these companies and their impact in the real world as competitive for the time and attention of their patrons.

On the topic of the business of self-publishing and the continuing shift from traditional publishing to indie, there are many great insights provided in this book. I found it incredibly helpful and inspiring that so many stories come from librarians that are also authors talking about their firsthand experiences.

Tom Bruno talks about one of my favorite Kevin Kelly articles that lays out an economic case for an artist being able to be supported by "1,000 True Fans." The article is a few years old now, but I was so excited when I initially read it that I immediately bought the domain name 1000truefans. com (I have yet to do anything with it). Tom provides an excellent overview of what the direct fan-to-creator relationship means to him (as an author), the emerging services to facilitate new ways of artists being paid, and other insights into the business of being indie.

Elizabeth Nelson gives an honest account of the better business deal offered by self-publishing, but makes clear there is a trade-off for the authors themselves taking on the responsibility and work. Not sugarcoating the realities of self-publishing is a great thing, and her piece accomplishes that well. Pushing the perspective of how the ground is moving underneath the traditional publishing industry, Joseph D. Grobelny talks about traditional authors who have begun to self-publish. The article is very insightful in recognizing this trend as a sign of things to come.

A few months ago, we hosted a Creator Day with our partners at the Massachusetts Library System (MLS), and we invited two self-published authors to speak to the librarians directly. We did not realize when we invited them that both were previously traditionally published authors who had opted to go indie on their latest books (one was a best-selling author who had appeared on Oprah, Rachel Maddow, and NPR's *Fresh Air*). Both felt like this was the direction the industry was going and had embraced this path. The librarians in attendance were surprised (and happy) to hear that these accomplished authors wanted to work directly with them and understood they could play a vital role in this new way of books reaching readers.

I was happy to see our own SELF-e project mentioned in several of the articles (self-e.libraryjournal.com). SELF-e is a partnership with *Library Journal* that is about 18 months old. SELF-e is well on the way to solving many of the problems and challenges presented in in this book. *Library Journal* has now curated thousands of self-published books that we are making available to patrons all over the country. And librarians themselves are starting to jump in the curation process as well. We now are working with several states and numerous leading urban libraries, each with a unique vision of how to apply our technology to solving their own local content access and curation issues.

The article included here from Melissa DeWild and Morgan Jarema at Kent District Library discussing about their curated local collections as part of the Kent Digital Library (KDL) is a great example of leadership in this area. Kent is clearly a library that understands how to leverage their brand and their ability to select books for their own audience. Any library looking to institute a local curation program can take a lesson from what they are doing with KDL.

I am deeply committed to the vision of independent publishing. The first 15 years of this revolution was about getting books into the world. In the past 15 years, millions of books have been self-published, which is a good thing. The next 15 years is about sorting and curating those books (and the books still coming from indie authors moving forward) and getting them in front of new, appreciative audiences.

Libraries are perfectly situated to perform this role partnering with software companies like BiblioLabs and others. As someone who has dedicated much of my professional life to the fulfillment of the true vision of indie publishing, I feel very fortunate to play a meaningful part in making this happen in the library world. And I feel very fortunate to be able to pen a few thoughts at the start of what I imagine will become a very important book on the road to fulfilling that vision.

Introduction to *Self-Publishing and Collection Development*

Robert P. Holley, Wayne State University

I first learned about the increasing importance of self-publishing not from an article in a library publication or even from a library blog or a discussion list. About three years ago on my way home from work, the woman on National Public Radio was talking about how around 75% of all titles published in the United States were self-published. As a teacher, researcher, and writer on collection development, I was amazed at this figure and wondered why I didn't know about this important development. Did librarians have their heads in the sand? Indeed they did, with a few exceptions.

Thus, I decided to find out more about this significant, but overlooked, development. My research over the last few years has led to several presentations, a special segment in *Against the Grain*, and now this book. I believe that it is the first monograph to deal with self-publication and its present and potential impact on libraries. Many librarians consider self-published or indie titles to be nothing other than the current manifestation of vanity press publications—those titles that authors paid to have printed only to sit in their basements or garages since bookstores wouldn't carry them and libraries turned them down even as gifts. All this has changed with e-books, print on demand, and Amazon and other Internet outlets. In fact, an industry has grown up to support these authors.

Both established authors with commercially published books and newbies have discovered the advantages of self-publication including higher royalties, complete control over content, and the ability to get things into "print" quickly. According to *Publishers Weekly*, 15 of the top 100 best

1

sellers last year were indie publications. Some authors have a loyal following with readers who want their libraries to purchase their books.

For libraries, the negatives of many self-published books are real. From the content side, many are poorly written with typos and formatting errors, have abysmal cover art, and are difficult to purchase especially if published only in a proprietary format. Practically, most of these books lack cataloging, don't receive reviews, aren't carried by the traditional vendors, and get minimal marketing except for the authors who want the local library to buy the book and/or sponsor a book talk. But beyond these difficulties, self-published books can meet the entertainment and information needs of users, the reason why libraries exist. The chapters that follow will discuss these points and many others. In any case, the sheer volume of these publications makes it impossible for libraries to ignore self-published books forever.

Public libraries are much further along in integrating self-published materials into their collections. Self-published books are more likely to be fiction with a strong emphasis on genre fiction, the type of pleasure reading that many public library users expect to find. Henry Bankhead describes the efforts of the Los Gatos Library to provide such materials and to support local indie authors in his "E-Book Self-Publishing and the Los Gatos Library: A Case Study." One special feature has been partnering with Smashwords whose headquarters are located in the same city. In "Supporting Self-Publishing and Local Authors: From Challenge to Opportunity," Melissa DeWild and Morgan Jarema focus on their efforts to make print publications by local indie authors available in the Kent District Library, Michigan. This library shelves indie publications in a separate section to increase their use and also sponsors a Michigan Authors' Night.

Kay Ann Cassell comes up with a less positive answer in her "Do Large Academic Libraries Purchase Self-Published Books to Add to Their Collections?' She includes cases where academic libraries buy such books, but they do so much less frequently than public libraries for many reasons, including the lack of reviews and vendor support as well as the fewer number of self-published scholarly publications. In "Why Academic Libraries Should Consider Acquiring Self-Published Books," Robert P. Holley then argues that academic libraries should take more interest in self-published materials because they can serve as primary sources, document popular culture, include research from independent scholars, and provide less expensive access to textbooks. Donald Beagle with "Digital Authoring, Electronic Scholarship, and Libraries: From Walled Garden to Wilderness" recounts his experiences both with commercial publishers and self-publishing. As an independent scholar, he sees the following advantages to self-publishing his research: the ability to make his findings available when the subject won't sell enough copies to justify commercial publication and complete control over content including eliminating unwanted publisher changes and providing more supplementary matter since e-books don't have the same size limitations as print publications.

Bob Nardini, ProQuest Books, and Robin Cutler, Ingram Publishing, deal with different aspects of vendors and self-publishing. Nardini ("Book Vendors and Self-Publishing") focuses more on selling to academic libraries with statistics that show that such sales occur but with a limited number of copies sold and a higher cost of doing business since such titles have higher handling costs without the support that traditional publishers provide. In her "Ingram and Independent Publishing," Cutler is more optimistic because IngramSpark, a support service for indie authors, has mechanisms in place to support sales to libraries and bookstores.

Eleanor I. Cook addresses the concern that self-published materials are less likely to be reviewed in "Review Sources of Interest to Librarians for Independently Published Books." She examines a broad array of reviewing sources in various categories that include Amazon.com, sites designed for readers, and traditional library and bookstore reviewing sources. While the sources that libraries use now contain some reviews, the percentage is much less than for commercially published materials. Robert P. Holley addresses another concern, the lack of cataloging/metadata for self-published materials, in "Self-Publishing and Bibliographic Control," an important issue since libraries use cataloging to help users find materials and for internal processes. The Library of Congress provides very few cataloging records so that libraries must depend upon vendors and other libraries to provide records or create their own original cataloging, an expensive process.

Self-published authors recount their experiences in the next four chapters. In "Self-Publishing and Libraries: The Slush Pile Is the Platform," Tom Bruno, tired of rejection letters, turned to self-publishing to make his work available. He also describes several models for self-publishing. AlTonya Washington calls herself "An Indie Author in a Library World." When a commercial publisher turned down the next title in her series, her choice was to self-publish. Based upon her experiences, she emphasizes reaching out to readers, including those readers who want to find their favorite authors in libraries. Elizabeth Nelson focuses on the process of getting her novel published in "The Romance of Self-Publishing." She discusses the options along the way and why she made the decisions she did. "Alacrity House Publishing LLC" is somewhat different because Frankie L. Colton founded her press to take advantage of the structures available to self-published authors. Her press has created several anthologies of local writing and also provides services to authors that wish to self-publish under this imprint.

The volume concludes with "Self-Publishing: A Bibliographic Essay" by Joseph D. Grobelny in which he provides a selective review of the literature on self-publishing. His essay provides access to articles that give additional information on the topics covered in this volume.

Overall, this volume presents the many facets of self-publishing. My hope is that readers will take self-publishing and indie authors more seriously as both an important trend and as a way to provide additional content of interest to their users. With money to be made, I predict that both the established players and creative entrepreneurs will figure out ways to make it easier for libraries of all types to discover, purchase, and make available self-published books.

1 | E-Book Self-Publishing and the Los Gatos Library: A Case Study

Henry Bankhead, Los Gatos Library

Language is a virus from outer space.
—William S. Burroughs

INTRODUCTION

I first met Mark Coker of Smashwords in about 2010 just before the iPad came out and a little before Amazon started offering the Kindle format for libraries. One of our library pages, the people who shelve the books, said to me: "Hey, Henry, you're into e-books. Do you know there is a major e-book publisher here in Los Gatos?" In response to my look of blank incomprehension, he told me about Smashwords. I then contacted Mark Coker who readily agreed to come to the library and do a presentation on e-books. Mark grew up in Los Gatos and had very warm recollections of using the Town Library as a child; he even remembered the name of his favorite librarian, Mrs. Jean Krcik.

What became immediately apparent as Mark was making his first presentation in the former Los Gatos Library building (we have since moved to a new building) was that Mark knew a lot about e-books and the commercial e-book market. At that time in 2010, figures from the International Book Publishing Association (IBPA) showed a marked increase in e-book sales. Smashwords was experiencing an equally significant increase in readership and book sales. What was also interesting about my initial meeting was that Mark knew very little about the challenges facing the library in terms of lending e-books. I realized conversely that librarians in general knew very little about the retail e-book market and even less about e-book self-publishing. This is significant because I think we each actually learned a lot from our differences in approach.

This chapter will seek to explain the context of Los Gatos as a community and the unique properties of Los Gatos Library. It will examine the plight of libraries with regard to local authors and examine the traditional library aversion to self-published work. We will try to understand the changing landscape of e-book self-publishing and why *indie publishing* is a more apt descriptor. We will learn about the genesis of the Smashwords–Los Gatos Library collaboration and about how it developed and how it functions. Finally, we will examine one of Los Gatos Library's latest self-publishing collaborations, the Community Publishing Partnership Initiative, and analyze the project from a cost-benefit perspective.

ABOUT LOS GATOS

Los Gatos is a small, affluent town on the edge of Silicon Valley in California where the median home price is well over a million dollars. The population of Los Gatos is about 30,000, and the Los Gatos Library's total operating budget is about $2.2 million. Thus library expenditures are about $73 per person. However, like most libraries in the state of California, Los Gatos Library participates in the state-sponsored universal borrowing program by which participating libraries issue cards to any resident of the state. In the past, before recent state budget cuts, this program monetarily compensated libraries that served patrons outside their area. With the loss of this program, however, the Los Gatos Library serves a significant portion of residents outside of its service area, particularly those from adjacent communities including the city of San Jose, without additional compensation.

The town of Los Gatos has a history of being a community focused on the arts, including the literary arts. This tradition extends back to the early part of the 20th century, as recounted by Bergtold (2004), when Los Gatos was home to writers including Ruth Comfort Mitchell, Kathleen Norris, and Charles Erskine Scott Wood, and into the mid-20th century, when John Steinbeck and Neal Cassady called the Los Gatos area home. The present-day town continues to embrace the literary arts: in 2011 the Town Council created the position of poet laureate of Los Gatos.

ABOUT LOS GATOS LIBRARY

Los Gatos Library is the smallest independent public library in Santa Clara County. Unlike adjacent counties in California, Santa Clara County does not have a unified library consortium to leverage economies of scale in providing library services. Instead the county is divided into one county library district that serves seven communities with the remaining communities of San Jose, Palo Alto, Sunnyvale, Mountain View, Santa Clara, and Los Gatos each running their own libraries or library systems. As such, Los Gatos is the smallest library with the least economy of scale. Los Gatos Library is conversely able to be more agile, especially in relation to the use of information technology, which has somewhat less of a burden in terms of cost and deployment in comparison with physical services. For example, the Los Gatos Library is a leader in the use of instant messaging, was the first library in California to deploy a mobile app through Boopsie, is one of a handful of libraries in California that use Mac computers for public computing, and was one of the first libraries in California to adopt open-source software for its library catalog and circulation system.

In addition, the town's local history is a featured part of the library collection. The former library director and a dedicated group of volunteers have amassed a large online collection of more than 8,000 documents and photographs featuring the town's history. This collection can be seen, in essence, as a form of library-as-publisher in that the library, in partnership with local volunteers and citizen providers, is creating free online access to its own database of library-created, "Web-published" material, some in the form of electronic documents. Where it differs from independent or self-publishing is its lack of connection to worldwide distribution channels and its lack of monetization.

ABOUT LOCAL AUTHORS

Traditionally, local authors have come to the Los Gatos Library to seek legitimacy for their work and to acquire readers. This generally has taken the form of authors presenting the library with a bound copy of their book that they have had independently printed for a fee. Though Los Gatos is a library that welcomes local author contributions, accepts donated copies of books from these authors, and has a local author section, not all libraries are able to do so. In addition, for Los Gatos Library, maintaining the local author section places somewhat of a burden on both the library and on the local author. The library is burdened by having to meet with each suppli- cant author, having to make a decision relating to the author's work based on the physical item being presented, and having to physically process and catalog the item and include it in the library collection. The burden on the author is both having to pay for the production of physical books and hav- ing to distribute these items. Local authors who try to donate electronic copies of their books have an additional challenge in that most libraries are unable to host their own e-books and instead rely on third-party providers who license and host e-books, though OverDrive recently implemented a local content-hosting feature to enable libraries to share e-book material with their patrons when the library retains the copyright (Valentine-Gold, 2013). Overall, there is a greater degree of efficacy for independent local authors to take advantage of free platforms such as Smashwords to publish their works as e-books that can then become available to the world via retail outlets such as iTunes and Barnes & Noble and to libraries by means of independent library e-book distributors and hosting services such as Over- Drive and Baker and Taylor.

STIGMATIZATION OF SELF-PUBLISHING

Traditionally libraries and librarians have taken a very dim view of what is known as self-publishing. This is in part because traditional publishing, centered on the major New York publishing houses, has been the arbi- ter of quality in the writing world. If the book was good enough, then the author would be able to secure a publisher to publish it. A publishing deal became the hallmark of success. The very concept of publishing, the mean- ing of "being published," revolved around this traditional model. Part of the essence of this model was the role of the publisher as a filter to guarantee quality. It's not surprising, given the examples detailed by Leddy (2007) of an editor such as Max Perkins in relation to major 20th-century authors such as Thomas Wolfe, Ernest Hemingway, and F. Scott Fitzgerald. The example of Gordon Lish and Raymond Carver, explored by Hemmingson (2011), also comes to mind. In these cases, the editors, and by extension the publishers, can be seen as having a very active role in the success of their writers. In some cases, their editorial contribution to the written work was possibly instrumental to the author's success. Thus, the stigma attached to authors who do not conform to the overall framework for deciding quality derives from these authors not passing through the approval process and engaging in the traditional publisher-author relationship.

The possibilities offered by worldwide Internet distribution have led to the breakdown of the relationships within traditional publishing and provide alternative paths to success for authors. An additional benefit for libraries and readers is 24-hour access to the library's collection of e-book materials. The author-editor relationship and, with it, the possibility for collaboration and quality control still exists, but in a different form, independent of the overarching organizing influence of the publishing house. This is not to say that completely unmediated e-book publishing does not occur, but the assessment of quality has migrated away from the traditional means of production and toward the consumer of the written work through the independent agency of the author. Thus, it becomes more the responsibility of the writer to seek editors and first readers rather than the job of the traditional publisher.

THE DISTINCTION BETWEEN SELF-PUBLISHING AND INDIE PUBLISHING

It can be said that the e-book "self-publishing" model has broken apart the model of traditional publishing and reassembled it into a new set of relationships. Because online e-book publishing and the rise of e-books have created a virtually free alternative to traditional print publishing, the very concept of e-book self-publishing must be reconsidered. With relation to e-books, "self-publishing" seems more descriptive of the physical model of the vanity press, where authors, hell-bent on seeing their book in print at any cost, would agree to pay up front to produce a physical product and then themselves take on distribution responsibilities. In the electronic realm, with platforms such as Smashwords and Amazon, the term *self-published* does not quite apply. Distribution is achieved by the platform and its connection to a multitude of worldwide distributors such as iTunes, Barnes & Noble, Flipkart, and so on. Best practices and style guidelines are also instituted and shared by the platform. Therefore, the term *independent publishing* or *indie publishing* is a better term to describe this process as many of the functions of the e-book publishing process are not in this case being performed by the author. Through the rise of electronic formats and electronic distribution, the integrated, multifaceted book production pipeline represented by traditional publishing has been deconstructed and reassembled. Layers of approval and control have been removed; instant access to a massive distribution pipeline has taken their place.

A MATTER OF SHIFTING RELATIONSHIPS

Interestingly enough, the success of self-publishing derives from a set of relationships. Though traditional publishing stresses the relationship between publisher and client, indie publishing has taken that relationship and turned it on its head. Control has migrated from publisher to author. Proportional profit sharing favors the author in the same way with the author receiving up to 80% of the sale price. The hierarchical structure of the traditional print-based business model has been transformed into a decentralized network. The example of "The Cathedral and the Bazaar" provided by Raymond (1999), developed to describe the efficacy of software development in an open-source environment, applies well to this case. In the traditional publishing model, the publishing house is represented by the idea of the cathedral, a hierarchically controlled machine that is engineered to a specific and highly defined purpose. Indie publishing is represented by the bazaar, similar to the open-ended collaborative environment in open-source software development; the bazaar is predicated on an organically developed set of peer-to-peer relationships in an unregulated and free-flowing environment. The context of indie publishing is this bazaar of possibility. Independent authors are able to choose from an array of free tools to produce their works as e-books and propagate them to reach a worldwide audience, thereby building direct readership and sales based on their direct connection to the marketplace or, in other words, the bazaar.

LOS GATOS LIBRARY–SMASHWORDS PARTNERSHIP: CO-PROGRAMMING

Initially, when we found out about Smashwords, the Los Gatos Library wanted to provide e-books from Smashwords to our library patrons. However, in 2010, Smashwords' books were not available through the main library e-book distributor, OverDrive. Since this was the main vendor we were using and because we, like most libraries, lacked an independent e-book hosting system, we decided to partner with Smashwords on library programming directed at local authors. This coincided well with the open-ing of the new Los Gatos Library and was aimed at illustrating the benefits of free e-book publishing tools for authors. Smashwords and Los Gatos Library staff worked together to present a set of three programs.

The first of these programs was intended to provide a general over-view of the e-book marketplace and of e-books available through the public library. Members of the public who attended this program learned about the different types of e-books available through the library. A few patrons were initially confused about the concept that an e-book could be "checked out" and not be available until it was "returned." For digital objects, this concept seems counterintuitive and somewhat illogical. This arrangement, called the "one book, one user model," seeks to mimic the model of physical book checkout. When it was explained that e-books the library purchased under this model (almost exclusively from OverDrive) cost about four or five times the normal retail price but were available "forever," the model made somewhat more sense. In addition, it was explained how this model benefits the large publishers. By contrast, during the self-publishing over-view part of the program, it became clear why the library was interested in self-published e-books as they typically cost much less, averaging $2.99.

The second program in the series was a basic treatment of e-book self-publishing and was called "A Primer on E-Book Self-Publishing." This pro-gram was completely run by a Smashwords staff member and Smashwords author, Angela Schiavone. Angela gave the audience a general understand-ing of what is involved in publishing an e-book. Being an author herself, Angela was able to address author concerns about self-publishing in relation to traditional publishing as well as provide general information about how self-publishing at Smashwords works. Most significant was the information that, unlike in traditional publishing where books have a narrow window for success before they are taken out of print, self-published e-books never go out of print. This means that authors have an indefinite amount of time to try to make their books successful.

The third program was a follow-up on the second and was entitled "E-Book Self-Publishing Best Practices." It provided a set of tips and tricks on using Smashwords, based on the practices of the most successful Smash-words authors. Topics included pricing models and thoughts on cover design (because readers do judge a book by its cover), as well as overall marketing strategies. Local authors also had time to ask questions, such as whether self-publishing would affect their potential for success with traditional publishers. Based on the attendance and questions asked during these sessions, the local author community was and still is extremely interested in learning more about e-book self-publishing.

LOS GATOS LIBRARY–SMASHWORDS PARTNERSHIP: CO-BRANDING

After our new library opened and after our initial series of programs, Los Gatos Library and Smashwords decided to launch a co-branded Web portal as a way to point local authors in Smashwords' direction. This was based on another co-branding portal that Smashwords had developed with the now defunct Sony Reader Store. The thinking was that authors who were using the Sony Reader Store or the library catalog would respond to messaging about the free tools of self/indie publishing. A co-branded link page would then lead them to the Smashwords Web site where they could access step-by-step information about how to create their own e-book and market it to a worldwide audience. So far only about 20 authors have opted to use the branded portal to create accounts in Smashwords. The Seattle Public Library replicated this concept in 2014 and has had more than 100 author sign-ups.

The ethos of the Los Gatos Library's partnership with Smashwords has been in somewhat marked difference to other library self-publishing initiatives. The "invisible hand," explained in Smith (1776), applies to our case because the library is seeking to let the marketplace decide the success or failure of any particular work. Our approach can also be seen as based on a "tough love" or "sink or swim" approach. The Los Gatos Library is not seeking to shepherd local authors into e-book self-publishing or, by extension, to directly acquire locally produced e-books to be part of the library collection. Rather, Los Gatos Library is pointing out the tools available for success to the community and encouraging authors to engage with those tools to publish e-books to a worldwide audience and to have those e-books disseminated by online distributors, including library e-book distributors. These books can then migrate back to the library as part of our regular materials selection process for considering e-books for purchase. The library can step out of its traditional role as curator and instead can look for and independently evaluate local content in the catalog of library e-book distributors.

SELF-E PARTNERSHIP

Los Gatos has also partnered with BiblioLabs and *Library Journal* to offer local authors the ability to submit their self-published e-books and opt to have them assessed by an expert panel of curators from *Library Journal* as described by LaRue (2015). This model, called SELF-e, contrasts to the Smashwords partnership in that, instead of letting popularity and the market determine quality, a panel of experts chooses certain titles for promotion. This quasi-contest model is somewhat similar to the model developed by the Reaching Across Illinois Library System (RAILS), the Soon to Be Famous Illinois author project, described by Erikson (2014). Our project seeks to energize local authors to submit content to a contest judged by experts where authors who are selected will receive accolades and attention. This bears some resemblance to the traditional publishing model, in terms of the external gatekeeper as the definition of success, but is different in that it takes place in a context of the celebration of the self-publishing phenomenon.

COMMUNITY PUBLISHING PARTNERSHIP INITIATIVE

The third phase in the Los Gatos Library–Smashwords partnership involves working together with local community partners to invite the entire community to join together to publish e-books. The initiative is called Community Publishing Partnership and started with collaboration among Smashwords, Los Gatos High School English Class 9H (taught by Tonya McQuade), and the Los Gatos Library. The collaboration started with an initial meeting among Mark Coker of Smashwords, Tonya McQuade, and me, Henry Bankhead. We discussed a framework for using the free self-publishing tools at Smashwords to teach the English class about self-publishing. This learning experience was built around the concept of encouraging all the class members to write original poems and contribute them to a jointly published anthology. All the members of the class became published authors and learned about the publishing process as a result.

MOBILE SELF-PUBLISHING LABS

The Community Publishing Partnership was also supported by an Innovation Grant from the Pacific Library Partnership, a San Francisco Bay Area library mega-consortium that is a consolidation of four library systems serving the counties of Alameda, Contra Costa, San Francisco, Monterey, Santa Cruz, San Benito, and Santa Clara. This grant, entitled Community Publishing Partnerships, provided $15,000 to build two mobile self-publishing labs to be used to support community groups such as the Los Gatos High School class in producing and viewing their e-books. Each lab consisted of one Mac Air laptop, 10 iPads, and an iLuv charging station as well as Microsoft Office for all of the devices. The role of these mobile labs varies according to the needs of our community partners. For the high school groups, the iPads provided a focus around which enthusiasm for the project was built. The iPads and laptop were not crucial for the project to occur but provided extra resources that the class could and did take advantage of. In a sense, the provision of the mobile labs was a way to create buy-in from the participants.

ENGLISH CLASS 9H

After the initial meeting among representatives from Smashwords, the library, and the high school, Tonya McQuade organized a series of class visits to introduce the self-publishing project to her three freshman English classes and to three classes of another freshman English teacher, Mrs. Kathleen Wehr. Mark Coker and I visited six classes in one day to explain the project, e-book self-publishing in general, and the role of the library in the project. A few weeks later, Mark visited all six classes again to give them a follow-up presentation on the best practices of e-book self-publishing.

After writing their original poems, the class broke up into functional teams to put the anthology together. This gave the class experience in the collaborative work that would occur in any business group working toward a common goal. The teams were designated as Layout and Design, Editing, Marketing and Publicity, Art and Photography, and Event Planning. The Layout and Design team divided the poems into thematic sections. The Editing team compiled the submissions from the entire class into one document, corrected spelling mistakes, and sought to format the document correctly for conversion to an e-book. The Marketing team met with Jim Azevedo, the publicity manager at Smashwords, who helped them craft a professional press release. The Art and Photography team used the iPads provided with the self-publishing lab to take photos of original artwork to serve as section headers for the book. The Event Planning team met with library staff to plan a book release party in the library. The entire project was accomplished in six weeks; and upon release the book reached #1 in the iTunes poetry category, the same day that the library hosted a standing-room-only book release party.

NEW TECH PROGRAM

The Los Gatos High School New Tech program, a technology-enhanced, inquiry-driven program where students engage in project-based learning, also published two additional anthologies of short stories on the Smashwords platform. The students from the New Tech program were able to replicate the success of the partnership with Smashwords, Los Gatos High School, and the Los Gatos Library. Their two anthologies of short stories were titled *Stories to Remember* and *Collection of Inspirational Teenage Stories.* In the collaboration with this high school cohort, Smashwords staff member Angela Schiavone went through a step-by-step demo for the class by showing some of the exact steps involved in formatting a Word document and uploading it to Smashwords. As part of this demo, the students learned the importance of cover art, the function of a table of contents in an e-book, how to avoid copyright infringement, and the function of the nine different e-book formats that the Smashwords platform produces by default upon the upload of a well-formatted Word document.

TRAIN THE LIBRARIANS

The next partners in this community publishing initiative were other local librarians. Mark Coker from Smashwords and Henry Bankhead hosted a librarians' workshop in September 2014 to introduce San Francisco Bay Area librarians to the community publishing concept. This event took place at the Mountain View Library. Henry Bankhead and Mark Coker presented the story of the collaboration between Smashwords and the Los Gatos Library and explained the evolution of the Community Publishing Partnership Initiative. Mark Coker provided an overview of the e-book indie publishing marketplace as well as a demonstration on creating a well-formatted Word document for conversion into an e-book using the Smashwords platform. One of the mobile self-publishing labs was provided by Los Gatos Library for the workshop and was lent to Mountain View Library for use in an upcoming program.

LIBRARY DISTRIBUTORS OF SMASHWORDS CONTENT: COMPLETING THE CIRCLE

As mentioned above, Smashwords titles initially were not available through any library distributors until the Baker and Taylor 360 access platform added them in 2012. Unfortunately, this platform was not from one of the vendors Los Gatos Library worked with. It was not until the ENKI independent platform, hosted by Califa and Contra Costa County Library System and described by Enis (2013), became available to Los Gatos Library that we were able to give our patrons any access to Smashwords content. In addition, ENKI offered libraries the opportunity to own their own e-books outright rather than just licensing them from major distributors. Initially the Los Gatos Library did not have the ability to purchase its own titles on ENKI; this feature was added in 2014, completing the circle for local authors. Thus an author could discover Smashwords through the library, then publish an e-book through the Smashwords platform, and then potentially see that book available through our online library catalog.

LIBRARY DISTRIBUTORS OF SMASHWORDS CONTENT: OVERDRIVE

The integration of Smashwords content with OverDrive, Los Gatos Library's main distributor of licensed e-book content, happened in mid-2014 after a long delay. With this integration, Smashwords content, including content from local authors, became available to Los Gatos Library patrons through the OverDrive platform. This is significant because OverDrive has the greatest presence in the library e-book distribution and hosting market. After the integration finally happened, an article appeared in *Library Journal* by Enis (2014), touting the benefits of the integration for libraries, readers, and authors. Initially, it was discovered that, in the OverDrive Collection development interface, branded as Content Reserve, the Smashwords content had been isolated in a self-published tab as observed by Giammatteo (2014), which was not searchable through the default search interface. This meant that librarians searching for Smashwords or self-published content would have additional difficulty in locating it if they did not know in advance that they had to select a particular tab before being able to search the content. At the same time, authors were becoming aware that their works were being "ghettoized" in OverDrive by being placed in a relatively hidden spot in the librarian's shopping interface. This was somewhat disconcerting and demoralizing for authors who had chosen to go with Smashwords rather than other indie publishers in order to get their books into library e-book collections through OverDrive. It must be assumed that OverDrive took authors' and librarians' concerns about this matter somewhat to heart because, as Hoffelder (2014) points out, a limited number of Smashwords titles have shown up in the main e-book catalog provided by OverDrive to libraries.

COST-BENEFIT ANALYSIS

Costs

Los Gatos Library is a small, agile organization without an active board. Instead, the Los Gatos Library is one of the departments of the Town of Los Gatos and has a wide degree of latitude to experiment with new programs and technology. Examples of this experimentation and risk taking include the following: Los Gatos is one of the few libraries that offer iMac computers for public computing; Los Gatos employs the use of improv-based role playing to model common staff-patron interactions and to improve overall customer service; Los Gatos has done away with the traditional Adult, Youth, and Technical Services departmental structure and instead implemented two basic teams—one that handles content and one that deals with infrastructure. Within this paradigm, collaboration with e-book distributors such as Smashwords and with the local high school is not something that ever required approval but instead is the expected behavior in an organizational culture of adhocracy as seen in Mintzberg and McHugh (1985). Therefore, the cost in a sense must be computed in staffing hours by totaling hours devoted to outreach and professional communication such as conference presentations and webinars related to the ongoing partnership as well as time spent lobbying OverDrive to integrate Smashwords content. This cost becomes somewhat nebulous as it is subsumed within the overall job descriptions of the employees, both hourly and administrative, who are involved.

Benefits

The benefits are much less nebulous and much easier to quantify. The success of publishing an original e-book anthology of poetry in conjunction with the high school speaks for itself. In a time when public libraries are challenged to look outward and build partnerships with the community, a successful project with the local high school that receives nationwide attention, as described by Mei (2014), is a significant achievement. The school partnership model is being continued with a freshman class from the 2014–2015 school year, building on the success of the previous year. Additional benefits are found in the number of local authors that have published through the Los Gatos Library–Smashwords portal: a total of eight books for the years 2013 and 2014 on Smashwords and two through the SELF-e platform for a total of 10. This may seem like a small number, though it should be noted that this number of books represents just the authors who opted to use the library portal to publish and also represents a subset of the 21 initial sign-ups through the portal. Also, despite the seemingly low usage of the portal, who is to say what effect any single self-published book may have in terms of readership? Even one successful book may have a great impact. In addition, the recognition in *Library Journal* of the author, Henry Bankhead, as a 2014 Mover Shaker for his support of self-publishing at the Los Gatos Library, as observed by Enis (2014), can be seen as a benefit in drawing attention to the project, to the concept of library self-publishing partnerships, and to the Los Gatos Library on a nationwide level. Also significant is the fourfold increase in e-book lending at the Los Gatos Library over the last two years (e-book checkouts for June 2013 totaled 320 while e-book checkouts for April 2015 totaled 1,248).

CONCLUSION

Los Gatos Library's partnership with Smashwords has evolved over time by progressing from co-programming to co-branding to the community publishing initiative. Los Gatos Library's collaboration with the Los Gatos High School and Smashwords to bring indie e-book publishing into the classroom remains the most significant aspect thus far in our promotion of e-book publishing. This is because it engages multiple community partners and many individuals to participate in and create a shared learning experience. The overall result of the work that Los Gatos has done with Smashwords to promote the free tools of e-book indie publishing has been to spark a fair amount of interest in the greater library community. Mark Coker and Henry Bankhead have presented two webinars and two conference presentations on the subject. The amount of professional interest in the subject may be due to the challenges facing libraries in relation to providing access to e-books from traditional publishers as well as the groundswell of interest nationwide in self-publishing as an alternative to the traditional commercial publishers. In addition, the movement for libraries to become loci for creation in addition to consumption, that is, the Makerspace movement, has played a significant part in the rise of interest in e-book self-publishing centered on the public library. This is particularly apropos as libraries are uniquely poised to offer all the tools needed for the public to engage in writing and, by extension, self-publishing: word processing software, computers, Internet access, books about writing, and spaces for community workshops. I have hopes that this volume and other works on self-publishing will get libraries of all types thinking about self-published or indie-published materials, to understand why they are important for libraries, and to find way to integrate them into their collections.

REFERENCES

Bergtold, P. (2004). *Los Gatos*. Charleston, SC: Arcadia.

Enis, M. (2013). Technology: Califa launches Enki for ebooks. *Library Journal*, *138*(11), 24.

Enis, M. (2014). Publishing: Smashwords, OverDrive pair. *Library Journal*, *139*(11), 21.

Erickson, S. (2014). Heating Up! *ILA Reporter*, *32*(5), 21–29.

Giammatteo, G. (2014). Building a library presence with Smashwords and Over-Drive [Web log]. Retrieved November 2014 from http://giacomogiammatteo.com/2014/07/smashwords-overdrive/

Hemmingson, M. (2011). Saying more without trying to say more: On Gordon Lish reshaping the body of Raymond Carver and saving Barry Hannah. *Critique*, *52*(4), 479–498. http://dx.doi.org/10.1080/00111610903379974

Hoffelder, N. (2014) Ebooks distributed by Smashwords now showing up in Over-Drive's main ebook catalog [Web log]. Retrieved November 2014 from http://the-digital-reader.com/2014/10/03/ebooks-distributed-smashwords-now-showing-overdrive-main-ebook-catalog/#.VHuI_KVor4I

LaRue, J. (2015). SELF-e comes to Cuyahoga. *Library Journal*, *140*(1), 1.

Leddy, C. (2007). The complicated writer-editor relationship. *Writer*, *120*(12), 8.

Mei, Y. (2014, May 19). California town librarian leads project for students to publish poetry ebook. Retrieved May 1, 2015, from http://www.slj.com/2014/05/teens-ya/california-town-librarian-leads-project-for-high-schoolers-to-publish-e-book/

Mintzberg, H., & McHugh, A. (1985). Strategy formation in an Adhocracy. *Administrative Science Quarterly, 30*(2), 160–197.

PR Newswire. (2012, March 2). Baker & Taylor to offer Smashwords ebooks in Blio ereading application and Axis 360 digital media library platform. *PR Newswire US.*

Raymond, E. (1999). The cathedral and the bazaar. *Knowledge, Technology & Policy, 12*(3), 23.

Smith, A. (1776). *An inquiry into the nature and causes of the wealth of nations.* Raleigh, NC: Alex Catalogue.

Valentine-Gold, H. (2013). Local content in OverDrive marketplace. *OverDrive Blogs* [Web log]. Retrieved November 2014 from http://blogs.overdrive.com /general/2013/09/17/local-content-in-overdrive-marketplace/

2 | Supporting Self-Publishing and Local Authors: From Challenge to Opportunity

Melissa DeWild and Morgan Jarema, Kent District Library

Libraries are an ideal place to write: they often offer quiet spaces, free wi-fi, and research information in convenient and accessible locations along with the added inspiration of being surrounded by books. It's no surprise that people seek the library as a place to write. They become "regulars," greeted each day by the library staff. They ask staff to help them find that arcane bit of information that will add depth and authenticity to their book. Eventually some of them even bring in the finished book and suggest that the library put it on the shelf for others to enjoy, but that's where the author may hit a roadblock with staff.

At the Kent District Library (KDL) in Kent County, Michigan, the first time a self-published book was sent to the collection development department for consideration about adding it to the library's collection, our initial response was not to add it. The book cover featured a man in what appeared to be a contemporary T-shirt even though the book was set during medieval times. The back cover offered a dense description of the story that did not encourage reading the book itself. This book did not have the kind of appeal that most books we purchased required, and it would have taken a cataloger significant time to create an original record for it to have been able to add the book to our system. The book, however, had a note attached with a plea from branch staff to please add it to the collection because the nice author had spent the past year using their branch as a writing office. We relented, made an exception, and sent the book on for cataloging. While it didn't circulate much, the author was incredibly happy and grateful for the library's support.

Whether authors use the library for a space to write and consult with staff, or they are simply patrons using the library to check out books or bring their kids in for story time, they appreciate the library. This is a place they love, and its main purpose is to provide books for people to read. Of course, they immediately think it's also the perfect place to feature their book—on the shelves or in a program.

Traditionally published authors have the benefits of editors who help make the book more cohesive and typo free, graphic designers who create a beautiful cover, experienced marketing departments to promote the book, and established avenues to gain exposure for the book through professional review sources. Staff who select books for libraries rely on this vetting process. They know what to expect with a book from a traditional publisher and usually have efficient workflows in place to discover and order these titles. These books show up in the electronic carts that vendors send and can be viewed in the vendor's database with publisher annotations, BISAC information, warehouse quantities, sales demand, book covers, and often reviews. This all helps to inform selection decisions. Once items are selected, it's then very easy to upload them into an acquisitions system to send and track orders.

On the other hand, self-published books can be full of typos and have confusing storylines or unappealing covers. It's not always obvious who the audience for the book is either. Should it be shelved in juvenile or teen fiction? With no reviews, staff may have to read the book themselves to determine the appropriate age for the content. Often the library's usual vendors won't have the book for sale, which means disrupting an efficient workflow to manually order the title. Most likely the book will also need original cataloging, requiring higher level cataloging staff and a significant amount of time. These factors along with limited staff time can make it difficult to easily add self-published books to the library's collection. Most libraries also don't have enough staffing to spend time finding the needle of self-published gems among the rougher manuscripts in the haystack.

When there were just a few local self-published books to consider adding to the collection, it was fairly easy to manage them. Then self-publishing took off in a dramatic way. A recent analysis of U.S. ISBN data by ProQuest affiliate Bowker showed that the number of self-published titles in 2012 jumped to more than 391,000, up 59% over 2011 and 422% over 2007. We were inundated with local authors dropping off their self-published books for the library to add to the collection or contacting staff asking them to purchase the title. Staff accepted the donated books with the caveat that we couldn't guarantee that they'd be added to the collection and that they could end up in the book sale. This reaction obviously did not engender happiness in our patrons. We needed a better way to support patrons while acknowledging the limits of library staff time and the collection budget.

A few of our library staff met and brainstormed how we could turn the current negative situation that staff and patrons were experiencing regarding self-published books into something more positive and supportive. Out of this, KDL's Local Indie collection was created. The collection features books that are either self-published or published by small, independent publishers. It also includes music CDs and DVDs from local musicians and filmmakers. West Michigan authors and artists may submit donated copies of their works with a Local Indie form found at www.kdl.org/localindie. The form gives details on the collection and how to submit items along with requiring the donor's contact information and details about the items in case the library decides to purchase additional copies. The library does reserve the right to decide not to add an item, although so far we have added all titles received. In order to lessen the impact on staff time, we create brief bibliographic records to catalog the items and classify them all as "local" in the call number rather than assigning a genre or age level.

The Local Indie collections are prominently displayed near the entrances of two of our largest branches. Before developing this collection, we found that self-published titles shelved in the regular collection were often ignored. We have large collections; and, without author name recognition or publisher marketing, these books just did not attract attention from patrons. Now they are identified as local, which draws interest, and occupy prime real estate in the library on display shelves. Staff also post reviews of these items on our blog in order to highlight them.

The collection now boasts about 300 titles. The most popular titles so far include a cookbook, a memoir, an adult fiction title, and a music CD from a popular local band. The title with the most circulation is *Tasting and Touring Michigan's Homegrown Food: A Culinary Roadtrip* by Jaye Beeler with photography by Dianne Carroll Burdick. Our next steps with this collection are to consider expanding it to additional branches and to explore ways to offer a digital version of the Local Indie collection.

KDL also occasionally purchases nonlocal self-published books. Print books are shelved with the regular collection, and e-books are available through OverDrive (via Smashwords). Generally the purchase is due to a request for the title from a patron. We consider the requests in light of our general collection policy, so it should be something that has broader appeal than one reader and is a good fit for our popular materials collection. The majority of the requests are for teen and adult genre fiction, especially romance and mystery. Some traditionally published authors such as Jessica Beck and Jennifer Ashley are now publishing new series installments themselves, so we have sought some of these potentially popular titles. For now, relying on patron requests to add nonlocal self-published materials has been the best way for library staff to discover the titles; it also guarantees some demand.

Beyond purchasing their self-published works, KDL has sought more options to support these authors. In 2012, KDL launched a free, full-day Writers Conference (http://www.kdl.org/events/go/writers_conference) that in its second and third years has attracted nearly 200 writers and includes sessions on traditional, independent, and self-publishing. Self-publishing sessions have included marketing, trailers, finding an editor, staying motivated, social media, and e-book publishing.

The growing number of self-published books has also brought an increase in requests to libraries to host local author events. As these can often be more sparsely attended than authors and libraries would like, particularly when figuring staff time invested in promoting and creating promotional materials for a single-author event, KDL is partnering with a locally based independent bookstore to host and cross-promote book signings, readings, and other events involving area authors.

When KDL and Schuler Books & Music met to discuss such a partnership, we learned that bookstores also see lower attendance than they would like for local author events. To address this, Schuler has branded its periodic multiauthor events as "Local Author Nights" and has developed a set of guidelines aimed at boosting attendance and giving new, self-published authors practice marketing their books and their appearances. Kent District Library adopted the bookstore's guidelines, modifying them slightly to be applicable in the library setting, and has branded a seasonal "Michigan Authors Night" at four branches. Each of the four branches, which represent the four quadrants of our county-wide service area, will host a Michigan Authors Night on the same third Thursday of the month every year.

While Local Author Nights or variations thereof are commonplace for libraries and bookstores with varying but typically minimal success, our goal is not primarily to boost sales for these authors but to give them experience in self-promotion and personal appearances. It is our hope that the library is seen as a venue that fosters this growth; and, in doing so, sales may follow.

A call for authors to appear is put in our regular *eNewsletter* and on social media four times a year; we also keep a record of authors who have contacted us via other methods. Those who are interested are asked to fill out a form that includes basic information about their book, provide a high-resolution headshot and book cover image, donate up to four copies of their book (or CD) to KDL's Local Indie collection, and give us e-mail addresses of up to 25 people from their list of contacts to whom we can send a dedicated promotional piece advertising the event. Up to five authors who provide all requested information in a single response by the designated deadline are invited to be featured on the next Michigan Authors Night. For our first and second Michigan Authors Nights, KDL received more than a dozen inquiries; but only four authors sent in all the requested materials by the deadline, so the concern about having to turn authors away is so far unfounded. What we found instead was that, for whatever reasons, local self-published authors did not seem prepared to provide the marketing materials required for the library to effectively promote their book at the event. Rather than serving to "weed out" the newbies, we believe this experience helps local authors learn what is expected of them as well as how seriously our library system takes helping them publicize their success. In this way, the library also serves as a training ground of sorts for new authors by preparing them for future marketing efforts.

The format of the Michigan Authors Night is casual: each author has up to 30 minutes to introduce themselves, talk about their path to publishing or how they came to write about the subject matter, and do a short reading. Q&A is done at the author's preference, either at the end of each individual presentation or after all other authors have presented. Authors may sign and sell their books following the presentation. If they are unaware of Square or other methods of selling their books via credit or debit card using a plug-in device for their smartphones, this is another opportunity for the library to serve as a guide for improving the marketability of our local authors. Prior to the event, authors receive a second set of guidelines, which include recommendations on how to select a pivotal passage from their book—one that would induce readers to purchase a copy, the importance of familiarizing themselves with the presentation space, and a complete list of all promotional avenues KDL will utilize to publicize the event.

KDL also started the Write Michigan Short Story Contest in 2012 in partnership with area libraries and our local independent bookstore. Write Michigan is open to all state residents and allows story submissions in three categories—youth, teen, and adult. In 2012, the contest received 551 stories representing 155 zip codes throughout the state. In 2013, story submissions rose to 888, a 61% increase. All submissions are read by two readers (e.g., librarians, booksellers, and other book lovers) and rated with the top stories selected as semifinalists. The top 10 stories in each category are then judged by celebrity and community judges (mostly published authors). Finally, the public votes on the Write Michigan Web site (www.writemichigan.org), which gives the authors additional exposure and involves the community. Once the winners are selected, they are published in an anthology that is included in the library collection and sold at the local independent book-store. For most authors, this is their first-time publication.

The rise of self-publishing has certainly been disruptive to traditional publishers but also to libraries. In trying to be responsive to patrons and create a positive, supportive atmosphere for local authors, the Kent District Library has had to rethink policies, collections, and programs. Finding a way not just to accept local self-published authors, but actually to welcome them, invite them into the library, and help them hone their craft and their marketing skills, has resulted in a beneficial experience for the library and our patrons.

3 | Do Large Academic Libraries Purchase Self-Published Books to Add to Their Collections?

Kay Ann Cassell, Rutgers University

Self-publishing has always been an option, but it has been a small and mostly ignored part of the publishing world until recently, and then mostly for public libraries. In fact, there has generally been a stigma attached to a self-published book, particularly for academic libraries. They thought it meant that the book had been rejected by traditional publishers. But many well-known writers self-published their first books, such as Mark Twain, George Orwell, and Ernest Hemingway. There were always a few publishing companies that catered to authors who had written a book and needed a publisher but did not want to go through the usual channels. They were labeled "vanity presses." There were also authors who only wanted to write one book—a memoir, a collection of essays, a genealogy, a novel, a book of poetry, and so on. They planned to sell it or maybe give it away to friends, family, and their local library. But by 2008 the self-publishing world was exploding. Probably it was in large part due to the proliferation of e-books that let an author publish a book without the costs of printing and binding and to the print-on-demand world where books did not have to be printed in advance of sales. Distribution became easier and less costly. Many e-books were listed by Amazon and other vendors of e-books so they were relatively easy for interested readers to find. By 2014 Bowker reported approximately 460,000 self-published titles, up 17% over 2013.

The way large academic libraries select and acquire materials for their collections is somewhat different from smaller academic libraries. The size of their budgets makes the way they organize and spend their funds different. All materials cannot be acquired on a title by title basis even if they wanted to proceed that way. So most spend some of their funds through vendors who preselect materials for them in various subject areas. The vendors send the books to the library following the guidelines set by the library. It is understood that the library will accept most or all of the books selected. After having said that, even these larger libraries do some title by title selection. They are always looking to fill in gaps in their collections, to acquire materials on new subject areas, to acquire materials for special collections, and to acquire unique materials that will be of interest to their user community. Depending on the subject area, some subjects produce more self-published materials than others.

PUBLISHERS AND VENDORS

New publishing houses have emerged designed to publish books by indie authors. Among them are CreateSpace, Smashwords, Lulu, and Author Solutions. Some were quickly purchased by other publishers. Author Solutions was purchased by Penguin Random House and CreateSpace by Amazon. Apple also has the Apple iStore, which has launched Breakout Books. Simon & Schuster has launched its own self-publishing company in partnership with Archway Publishers, an Author Solutions imprint (Herther, 2013, p. 23). It is obvious from this wave of new publishing houses and then their mergers that traditional publishing wants to capture some of this writing talent for themselves as well as the profits self-publication generates. For example, Smashwords made $22 million in 2013 (*Inc.*, 194).

In 2013, Ingram developed IngramSpark to assist self-publishers and libraries. IngramSpark describes itself as a single platform for authors to publish and distribute their books—either e-books or print. If the authors choose e-books, Ingram will distribute them to Amazon Kindle, iBooks, Kobo, and other distributors. The authors can also choose print copies, and they will be provided through print on demand. Vendors such as Ingram are attempting to vet self-published material since all self-published material is not of the same quality. They are trying to identify titles of interest to libraries and help in the marketing of these titles. They stated that they are trying to build more metadata to increase discoverability. This is a big challenge. Yet to ignore this material means that some titles of interest go unnoticed and are not acquired. Bob Nardini from Ingram Library Services reported at the 2014 Charleston Conference about their efforts to vet these self-published titles. He said they had identified 380 titles of interest. They sold 12 copies of one book, and 15 copies of that title were listed in OCLC's WorldCat. Nardini said that publicity does help the sales. He mentioned one title, *Quack This Way*, which is an interview by Bryan A. Garner with David Foster Wallace. This book received a *New Yorker* review, and 33 copies of that title were listed in OCLC's WorldCat. Baker and Taylor has acquired Bookmasters, which offers similar services for self-publishers.

REVIEW SOURCES

When asked about acquiring self-published books, academic librarians often say that they don't want to buy them because they aren't reviewed. But this is no longer accurate. Although this was once the case, now many review tools include self-published books. I spoke to the staff of *Choice* where many academic librarians look for reviews. They told me that they will review self-published books if they follow the procedures outlined for submitting books for review. *Publishers Weekly* reviews self-published books on a regular basis. *Library Journal* now has SELF-e, which is a partnership with BiblioBoard. BiblioBoard is a platform for libraries to license and deliver digital content for an unlimited number of simultaneous users. The content includes e-books, articles, documents, and audiovisual materials. Many of its materials are primary source materials of special interest to academic libraries. Academic libraries can also use BiblioBoard to create online exhibits of special collections materials or for faculty to create e-textbooks. A new review source is *BlueInk Review* (www.blueinkreview .com). This fee-based review source uses professionals from the media such as the *New York Times* and the *Washington Post* and from major publishing houses to review self-published books. The reviews are well written, and the best books receive starred reviews.

THE AUTHORS

Some academic librarians may think that most of the material that is self-published is not written by academics or not written for the academic audience. This is not true at all. A recent article in *Inside Higher Ed* discussed the pros and cons of self-publishing for academics. The article stated that those academics who do not have tenure self-publish at their own risk.

Self-published monographs usually do not count when the work of an academic is considered for tenure. So nontenured faculty tend to try to find a traditional publisher to publish their work. Once the faculty member is tenured, there is more room for exploring alternate publishing routes. For many academics, the traditional publishing route is slow and causes authors to lose control of their material as they are asked to sign away all of their rights including the copyright. For most, there is not much money to be gained from traditional publishing unless the author writes a textbook or a book that can be used as a textbook that is adopted by many universities.

The conservative nature of much of the traditional publishing world sometimes makes self-publishing a better choice. For many, getting their book out to the public is preferable to dealing with the slow pace of traditional publishing that may not produce more income and may not even market the book very well. One can only judge this claim by the number of mid-list authors published by traditional publishers who are forced to do their own marketing. For those who choose the self-publishing route, it means that their work can be made available to everyone for no fee or for a small fee. It can be available much more quickly, and it can be listed with major outlets and platforms such as Amazon. It also means they must market their own work, which many do successfully thanks to social media. They can also create their own Web site that will help people find out more about the author.

Some faculty are now writing online textbooks, which are a new market and can be very successful. Online open-access textbooks have the advantage of making the author's work available to all at no cost or at a small cost and making revisions possible whenever needed. It can also mean that other faculty using the textbook can be engaged in the process of writing and revision so that the textbook can be a solid cooperative effort. At a recent conference, an academic gathered together some of the other faculty using his open-access textbook so they could offer suggestions as to what revisions and additions were needed. They charted a plan for getting revisions to the person coordinating the textbook so all points of view could be included in the next edition (Glushko, Petras, & Shaw, 2013). For others the self-publishing route gives them a chance to publish something that may be of interest but outside their specialty. They can then decide whether they want to add it to their CV.

LIBRARIES

Self-publishing has two separate meanings in libraries—acquiring self-published books and library involvement in publishing. Do academic libraries acquire self-published materials? The answer is "yes, but . . ." and "it depends." So maybe academic librarians don't often go out and look for self-published materials to acquire; but they do, in fact, acquire them on a case-by-case basis. Sometimes they buy them, and sometimes they are gifts. Librarians are now more open to self-published books because they often include content not available elsewhere. The problem is identifying them and finding a way to evaluate them if they have not been reviewed. The most often articulated reason for buying self-published books is that they were written by faculty, employees, or alumni of the institution. In this case, librarians know something about the author so they can judge whether the book is of reasonable quality or whether it should be purchased for political reasons. Librarians seldom refuse books that are local in nature. It is usually a good political and courteous move to accept these books and to add them to the collection. The next category of books that academic libraries often accept are books of local or regional interest. This might mean a book about the university, a book about the history of the area where the university is located, or a book of poetry or work of fiction by a local author. Once again, it makes good sense to have such books in the collection. Many libraries may have a local or regional history special collection and are looking for materials for this collection.

Librarians, as they look for material to add to a particular special collection or subject area, often find that the book that fits their collection is in fact a self-published book. Because some reviews and listings do not make any distinction as to whether the book is self-published, the librarian may have made a preliminary decision before realizing that the book is self-published. A colleague was kind enough to post a question about self-publishing on the listserv of the Literatures in English Section of ACRL. Here are some reasons given by academic librarians for adding self-published books. A library collects books on Barbados and the surrounding Caribbean area. Since there are not many publishers in this region, many books of interest are self-published, and the content is not available elsewhere. In another case, the librarian was looking for a play by John Roman Baker, a well-known contemporary British playwright. The play was available through Lulu, which distributes self-published material, but not available through any traditional publisher. In this case, the playwright self-published his play in order to make it available. In fact, the playwright has published three collections of his plays through Lulu. In another case, a university librarian in the Chicago area actively collects local zines, poetry chapbooks, and minicomics. Most of these are self-published, so the librarian is using other than traditional listings in order to acquire them. Another librarian said that the publishing scene had changed and that purchases would be considered on a case-by-case basis. As I inquired of other academic librarians as to whether they acquired self-published material, they first said "no"; but, after our conversation, many realized either that they do acquire self-published books from time to time or, if not, they were open to acquiring self-published books in certain subject areas. These areas included history, biography, genealogy, speeches, letters, diaries, essays, fiction, and poetry.

I identified a couple titles from Lulu that seemed interesting and perhaps worthy of being acquired by an academic library. One was *King Bridge over Troubled Waters* by Karen Van Etten, a book about the battle for the historic preservation of the King Bowstring Bridge in Newfield, New York. It seemed to be a relevant book for libraries interested in local history. In checking OCLC WorldCat, I found that the Cornell University Library owns it, thus showing their interest in local history even if self-published. The second one I selected was *Howardsville: The Journey of an African-American Community in Loudoun County, Virginia* by Kevin Grigsley. Once again a search of OCLC WorldCat showed at least six libraries that owned it. Although it was not surprising to see public libraries in Virginia owning this title, it was interesting to see that the Princeton University Library owned it as well as the Library of Congress. The third was *He Loved to Carry the Message: The Collected Writings of Douglas Helms* by Douglas Helms. Helms was a historian who was employed at the National Archives and at the U.S. Department of Agriculture. This self-published book is owned by Cornell University Library, the University of North Carolina at Chapel Hill Library, and the Library of Congress.

An article by Dilevko and Dali (2006) discusses their extensive research on the number of self-published books listed in OCLC. They determined that public libraries were buying more self-published books than academic libraries and that the largest category of self-published books being acquired by libraries was handbooks and manuals followed by history, biography, and autobiography. This study shows that pre-2006 libraries were already acquiring a great deal of self-published material.

Interestingly, one librarian said that he buys books through individual Web sites and through Kickstarter, which is a way of funding new projects including publishing. Joel Friedlander, a blogger and self-published author, says that "crowdsourcing has shown promise as a funding technique for authors with a compelling story and an ability to tell it well on video" (Herther, 2013, p. 24). Six thousand publishing projects were launched on Kickstarter in 2013 with $22.2 million pledged. Publishing projects have a 32% success rate (Reid, 2014, pp. 8–10). Other popular sources for funding self-published authors are Indiegogo (indiegogo.com) and Author.com (Herther, 2013, p. 24). Librarians give examples of buying self-published material based on recommendations from faculty. In this case, the faculty member knows the author personally or by reputation. Librarians do say that it is harder to decide about self-published material. They often have to buy it and then read it to make a final decision about including it in the collection if they are not familiar with the author's work.

The second role of self-publishing in libraries is publishing itself. This can be new material written by faculty and others on a university campus. These items may be published as books or as journal articles. Some libraries are involved in republishing their special collections material that is in the public domain. The University of Michigan, for example, is publishing monographs in print and electronic formats. They are reissuing materials from the University of Michigan collections. These materials include Center for Japanese Studies publications and the Michigan Historical Reprints Series. At Cornell University, the publications include an Islamic series. At Purdue, the library and the Purdue University Press worked together to save and reproduce digitally some transportation technical reports (Cook, 2014, p. 70). At SUNY-Geneseo, the library is publishing work from faculty and supporting a SUNY-wide textbook program (Cook, 2014, p. 70).

There is no doubt that libraries' and librarians' attitudes toward self-publishing are changing. The availability of more self-published titles makes selection more interesting and fills holes in collections. Well-researched books on relevant new topics are always welcomed by librarians. In sum, self-publishing is bound to have less and less negative effect on whether libraries acquire these books. This is not to say that there are not some advantages to traditional publishing. One possible reason for not seeing more interest in self-published material is that academic libraries have had decreases in their monograph budget so they are more reluctant to take a chance on what they view as an unknown quantity. Also, they are placing more emphasis on their institutional repositories and on digital materials. Joseph D. Grobelny, while discussing academic libraries in his article in *Against the Grain,* stated that "while many readers who look at the literature on the relationship between self-publishing and libraries might conclude that libraries will soon be left behind the market, it is worth taking the longer view that libraries will most likely successfully adapt to the changed publishing environment" (Grobelny, 2013, p. 36). Vendors and libraries will need to work together to identify high-quality self-published materials of interest to library users. They also need to encourage review media to review more self-published material. It is encouraging to see the number of review sources increase, which can only help to make new titles more accessible to academic libraries and to library users.

REFERENCES

Baverstock, A. (2012). Why self-publishing needs to be taken seriously. *Logos: The Journal of the World Book Community, 23*(4), 41–46.

Chart. (2014). *Inc., 36*(7), 194.

Cook, E. I. (2014). Preconference report. November 6, 2013. *Against the Grain, 26*(2), 70–75.

Crawford, W. (2013). Self-publish or traditional? My experience with books for librarians. *Against the Grain, 25*(3), 16, 18.

Dilevko, J., & Dali, K. (2006). The self-publishing phenomena and libraries. *Library and Information Science Research, 28*(2), 208–234.

Glushko, R. J., Petras, V., & Shaw, R. (2013). The discipline of organizing in ischools— collaborative and digitally enhanced teaching of a core subject. https://www.ideals.illinois.edu/handle/2142/47247

Grobelny, J. D. (2013). Self-publishing: A bibliographic essay. *Against the Grain, 25*(3), 35–37.

Hadro, J. (2013). What's the problem with self-publishing. *Library Journal, 138*(7).

Herther, N. K. (2013). Today's self-publishing gold rush complicates distribution channels. *Online Searcher, 37*(5), 22–26.

McCartney, J. (2015). A look ahead to self-publishing in 2015. *Publishers Weekly*, *262*(3), 36–38.

Montgomery, J. G. (2010). Group therapy—acquiring self-published books. *Against the Grain, 22(5)*. Retrieved from http://docs.lib.purdue.edu/atg/vol22/iss5/28

Nardini, B., & Schnell, J. (2013). Self-publishing: Breaking down barriers. *Against the Grain, 25(3), 32.*

Reid, C. (2014). Publishing campaigns grown on Kickstarter. *Publisher's Weekly*, *261*(20), 8–10.

Tyson, C. (2014). A publisher of one's own. *Inside Higher Ed*. Retrieved from www.inside highered.com/news/2014/07/17/self-publishing-option-academics-periphery?

4 | Why Academic Libraries Should Consider Acquiring Self-Published Books

Robert P. Holley, Wayne State University

Self-publishing now accounts for the majority of titles made available in the United States according to recent statistics, though sales volume is much less than for books from traditional publishers (Bowker). The increasing importance of e-books, coupled with the availability of print on demand, has made it possible for any writer to self-publish and to sell the resulting work on Amazon, Smashwords, Lulu, and other sites. Libraries are only beginning to grapple with this phenomenon. For libraries, many factors work against the acceptance of self-published books. While they do not have to be inferior to commercially published items, many are because of sloppy editing, typographical and grammatical errors, inferior content, and substandard illustrations and cover art. Most authors lack publishing experience; many are unwilling to pay for the services that would improve the quality of their productions. In addition, self-published materials do not fit in well with the established distribution channels for libraries. They often lack high-quality cataloging or quality metadata. The Library of Congress excludes them from the Cataloging in Publication program (Cataloging in Publication Program) and acquires and catalogs self-published works only in exceptional circumstances (Library of Congress). They are also much less likely to receive reviews in the publications that libraries consult, though this may be changing a bit. (See the chapter on review sources by Eleanor Cook in this volume.) Vendors find it difficult to stock these books and make them available to libraries, though some are trying. (See the articles on vendor support by Cutler and Nardini in this volume.) Overall, even libraries interested in self-published books will encounter difficulties in discovering, acquiring, and cataloging them.

THE PUBLIC LIBRARY

Public libraries are currently more likely to be grappling with the issue of self-published materials. The main reason is that one of the primary goals of public libraries is providing the recreational reading material that their patrons want. Avid readers of all sorts, but especially those with interests in genre fiction, require a steady stream of new books. The patrons are also likely to have encountered these items on Goodreads and other reviewing sites, some of which focus on reviewing self-published materials. In addition, they may follow blogs that give recommendations specifically for self-published books, often with a specialization in genre fiction. Public libraries with a policy of honoring all or most patron requests from traditional publishers may have a hard time explaining why they don't do the same for self-published works.

A second reason is that many authors who self-publish actively market to libraries. These authors can get advice from Web sites such as Stories to Tell on how to get their self-publications into stores and libraries ("Getting Your Self-Published Book into Stores and Libraries," 2014). For those interested in the topic, this blog entry also includes a short bibliography of other resources to consult. These marketing tools give suggestions not only on how to convince public libraries to purchase the author's book but also on how to ask to give a book talk. Finally, Smashwords has concluded an agreement with OverDrive to sell packages of e-books to libraries at very attractive prices of mostly less than $4.00 per title. Since most of these packages are fiction, public libraries are the intended audience (Smashwords, 2014).

ACADEMIC LIBRARIES

Academic libraries, on the other hand, still actively avoid purchasing most self-published materials. Bob Nardini in his chapter includes statistics on how few self-published books his company sells to American academic libraries. Kay Cassell comes to much the same conclusion in her chapter on the collecting patterns of large research libraries.

Why then should academic libraries collect self-published materials? Many believe that academic libraries of all types are interested only in serious, scholarly publications from reputable publishers since their editors and editorial boards help guarantee quality. While this statement is partially true, this chapter presents reasons why academic libraries should consider collecting self-published books to meet the immediate and especially long-term needs of their users.

Primary Source Material

Self-published books can be excellent primary source material. Issues of peer review and scholarly respectability do not apply to primary sources. Some of these self-published books may be a gold mine for future researchers seeking a more direct perspective from less skilled writers who publish items about their personal experiences and about topics where they have firsthand knowledge, such as autobiographies or personal narratives. The stories of a veteran who served several tours of duty in Iraq and Afghanistan could provide direct historical insights that might not appear in commercially published materials written by officers, politicians, and academics. Similarly, the personal story of growing up in the region where the library is located could be valuable for local history. The same would be true if the author is writing a biography of "dear Aunt Clara." In other words, these items are like the ephemeral materials that have appeared in many major microform/digital sets such as *Early English Books*. Academic libraries have spent thousands of dollars for these collections in which the majority of the items are not scholarly but are valued as primary sources.

Popular Culture

A second value tied to the first is that self-published materials can provide evidence of the popular culture of the era. Books that would never be commercially published can record the ideas of writers who are outside the publishing mainstream or do not belong to respectable scholarly communities. In addition, many of these writers would not be skilled enough to write a book acceptable to a commercial publisher. They are also willing to treat topics that the larger trade publishers would avoid. Thus, these books may provide some of the best source materials on popular culture trends such as creationism, Holocaust denial, antivaccination beliefs, and nontraditional sexual practices. Once again, quality is not the issue as much as the fact that they provide evidence about cultural trends that may not be respectable enough to be found elsewhere. If such self-published books are sold on Amazon, the researcher can also use the sales rankings to evaluate their resonance with the general reading public. The same could be true for fiction. For example, Amazon rankings for zombie books could provide statistical evidence for this subgenre's popularity beyond the sales figures from trade publishers.

Early or Later Works by Important Authors

50 Shades of Grey is an excellent example of a book that was originally self-published. The sales of an early self-published version of this book caused Random House to publish the book commercially and help it become a massive best seller. In his blog, Ronald H. Balson gives nine examples of this phenomenon (Balson, 2013). Right now, beginning authors may be self-publishing their first works years before becoming part of the literary canon. With the author's heightened future reputation, these earlier works will become interesting to scholars. Though perhaps less likely, the same might be true for a commercially published author who falls out of favor yet continues to self-publish. Finally, some reasonably important authors may decide to self-publish to gain the benefits from the higher royalty payments available to authors who eliminate the publisher as middleman or to escape the limitations imposed by commercial publication as discussed in the next category.

Independent Scholars

Under the term "independent" scholars are included both researchers without an academic affiliation and professors who for whatever reason are not worried about achieving the benefits of being published by a traditional academic publisher. One of the main reasons faculty, especially those on the tenure track, avoid self-publishing is that tenure and promotion committees seldom give much value to these publications (Tyson, 2014). The fact that a press, preferably a university press, accepted the manuscript is considered to be a sign of its scholarly importance. Senior tenured scholars, on the other hand, are apt to worry less about such considerations and be more interested in a wider dissemination of their ideas.

One principal reason for self-publishing is that some research is no longer economically viable for trade or university press publishers. Many scholars in the humanities and some social sciences create excellent scholarship but with such a narrow focus that few others are interested in the results. In the past, many university libraries automatically purchased all publications from university presses, but the decline in library resources coupled with the increasing importance of patron-driven acquisitions has greatly reduced the number of libraries that do so (Esposito, 2014). Self-publishing may be the only possibility for such manuscripts other than open access, which does not provide any economic reward for the author and does not get the broader distribution that Amazon and other sites provide.

A second reason is that self-publishing gives the author complete control over the book. With a traditional publishing contract, the scholar and the publisher may disagree over the shape of the final book. The scholar is perhaps interested in how to best present the research to peers while the publisher must look at production costs and sales potential that will depend upon a broader audience. The more marketable and accessible book may infringe upon what the scholar regards as its intellectual integrity. As recounted by Donald Beagle in his chapter on his publishing experiences, publishers may make cost-cutting decisions that work against the academic value of the work. In a virtual e-book environment, a scholar can control not only the content but the format of the text and can include as much supporting documentation, statistics, charts, illustrations, and photographs as she wants. While another option for authors is to include supporting documentation in a separate Web site, making this documentation available with the main text is a far preferable alternative. Finally, self-publishing allows the author to keep the book in print forever.

Textbooks

The potential ability to provide self-published textbooks may be the most exciting development for academic libraries. Libraries have traditionally not purchased textbooks because of their cost, frequent editions, and lack of original content. To quote the University of Georgia's *Collection Development Policy*: "In general, the Libraries' emphasis is on collecting works presenting new and original research or primary source material rather than textbooks" (University of Georgia Libraries, 2014). To deal with the increasing cost of textbooks that place a heavy financial burden on students, faculty are producing and self-publishing textbooks for their classes and for others in the field. For example, the *Wall Street Journal* recently published a column about an Econ 101 textbook that cost $250

(Richardson, 2015). Through self-publishing, faculty can consider creating their own textbooks at a much lower cost while still earning the higher royalties that self-publishing offers. Amazon, seeing the economic potential of these initiatives, has also announced plans to support textbook publishing ("Amazon Announces Self-Publishing Program for Education," 2015). With the much lower cost of these self-published textbooks, academic libraries may reverse their former policies against buying textbooks and thus satisfy one of the most important information needs for their students.

Comprehensive Collections

A final category is the question of the importance of self-published books for comprehensive collecting. In the past, particularly before the information explosion caused by the Internet, some of the largest research libraries collected as comprehensively as possible in some subject areas that they considered their specialties. The following is the definition for the highest level of the RLG Conspectus as listed on the Library of Congress Web site.

> Comprehensive Level: A collection which, so far as is reasonably possible, includes all significant works of recorded knowledge (publications, manuscripts, and other forms), in all applicable languages, for a necessarily defined and limited field. This level of collecting intensity is one that maintains a "special collection." The aim, if not achievement, is exhaustiveness. Older material is retained for historical research. In law collections, this includes manuscripts, dissertations, and material on non-legal aspects. (Library of Congress, "Cataloging and acquisitions")

Are there any large research libraries that still support this lofty goal for parts of their collections? If yes, will these libraries attempt to collect self-published books? There is nothing in this definition that excludes them except perhaps the word "significant," but as stated above at least some self-published books may have academic importance. A key issue for achieving comprehensiveness will be discovering nontraditional publications in the same way as it was in the predigital age. For the largest research libraries, a "free" item could be extremely costly because of the expensive bibliographer or curator time required to locate it. The Internet with its search engines has made it easier to find known items but has also created many more places to look for possible relevant discoveries. Scanning for important but unknown items is increasingly difficult with the great increase in the number of titles. Self-publishing may produce titles that are needles, perhaps even golden needles, in very large haystacks of worthless chaff. In addition, even the largest libraries in the world may be hesitant to take on the task of acquiring self-published materials even if they are valuable for current and future researchers in these times of diminishing resources for libraries. Comprehensive collecting may no longer be possible except for very narrow areas.

A FINAL ISSUE FOR ACADEMIC LIBRARIES

The discussions above have basically made the assumption that academic libraries should be interested in self-published materials from the United States and perhaps Canada and the United Kingdom. The second assumption has also been that these materials would be mostly in English. This chapter therefore overlooks the fact that self-publishing may include materials in other languages in these countries, particularly Spanish in the United States and French in Canada, and omits any consideration of self-publications from the rest of the world. This topic is an area for further research beyond this chapter's focus on what may be called traditional American self-publishing. Thus, the issue of self-publishing may be even larger than it has been framed in this discussion.

FINAL THOUGHTS

This chapter gives the reasons why academic libraries should consider collecting self-published works. Whether they will is a completely different matter. In this epoch of budget restraint, serials, databases, and "big deals" are taking an increasing portion of the collection development budget of all types of libraries. Many academic libraries do not have enough funds to purchase important books, even those published by university presses. Diverting money from these areas to collecting self-published materials would be difficult to justify without faculty and administrative support. In addition, several of the most important reasons, such as collecting primary source materials and the history of current popular culture, are most likely important for future users rather than for current research. Thinking of users in the next century while not buying what current users want immediately requires a leap of faith. In addition, self-published materials require more staff time to identify, purchase, and then catalog. (See my chapter on bibliographic control in this volume.) Staff time may be in even more short supply than money.

Having researchers, particularly faculty, request self-published materials would be the primary impetus for academic libraries to purchase them. Since most self-published books are quite inexpensive and sometime free, those researchers will be tempted to purchase them directly rather than ask the library to do so. The second most likely possibility would be for special collections librarians to seek self-published materials in those areas of particular interest that support their collection goals such as subjects comprehensively collected or books of local interest. These librarians are used to ferreting out difficult to find materials. A final possibility is less likely. Perhaps Smashwords would do for academic libraries what it is currently doing for public libraries: identify works of potential interest and then sell relatively inexpensive packages of materials of importance for academic libraries. The most likely candidates would be works of scholarly value published by independent scholars.

To conclude, self-publishing is still in its infancy. As stated above, public libraries are more aware of the meteoric growth in self-published titles; some have started to grapple with its implications. Academic libraries will need to do the same sooner or later or miss out on acquiring potentially valuable books for their collections.

REFERENCES

Amazon announces self-publishing program for education. (2015). Retrieved from https://www.insidehighered.com/quicktakes/2015/01/23/amazon-announces -self-publishing-program-education

Balson, R. H. (2013). Bestseller success stories that started out as self-published books. *Huff Post Books.* Retrieved from http://www.huffingtonpost.com/ronald -h-balson/bestseller-success-storie_b_4064574.html

Bowker. Self publishing in the United States, 2007–2112: Print and e-book: Bowker.

Cataloging in Publication Program. Frequently asked questions. Retrieved from http://www.loc.gov/publish/cip/faqs/#self_

Esposito, J. (2014). Revisiting demand-driven acquisitions. *The Scholarly Kitchen.* Retrieved from http://scholarlykitchen.sspnet.org/2014/10/15/revisiting -demand-driven-acquisitions/_

Getting Your Self-Published Book into Stores and Libraries. (2014). Retrieved from http://www.storiestotellbooks.com/blog/getting-your-self-published-book -into-stores-and-libraries.html

Library of Congress. Cataloging and acquisitions. Collecting levels. Retrieved http://www.loc.gov/acq/devpol/cpc.html

Library of Congress. Library and information science: A guide to online resources. Frequently asked questions. *Web Guides.* Retrieved from http://www.loc.gov /rr/program/bib/libsci/faq.html

Richardson, C. (2015, January 13). The $250 Econ 101 textbook: We economics professors are missing a chance to teach a cardinal lesson about the unchecked rise of prices. *Wall Street Journal (Online).* Retrieved from http://www.wsj.com/articles/craig-richardson-the-250-econ-101-textbook -1421192341?KEYWORDS=textbooks

Smashwords. (2014). Smashwords and OverDrive to bring 200,000+ indie ebooks to 20,000+ public libraries. Retrieved from http://blog.smashwords .com/2014/05/smashwords-and-overdrive-to-bring.html

Tyson, C. (2014). A publisher of one's own. *Inside Higher Ed.* Retrieved from https://www.insidehighered.com/news/2014/07/17/self-publishing-option -academics-periphery

University of Georgia Libraries. (2014, August 22). Collection development policy. Retrieved from http://www.libs.uga.edu/colldev/cdpolicy.html#Textbooks

5 | Digital Authoring, Electronic Scholarship, and Libraries: From Walled Garden to Wilderness

Donald Beagle, Belmont Abbey College

In the Age of Print, publishing was like a walled garden—authors gained admission if others (editorial boards, peer reviewers) judged their work to be worthy. If not, authors were kept outside and only then considered self-publishing, which was not considered very respectable. In the Digital Age, those walls are crumbling, and the garden becomes a wilderness. Print publishers see their economies of scale erode, and self-publishing is losing its stigma. Today, librarians will not necessarily find the best new scholarship laid out in an orderly manner. Some of the most exciting and innovative scholarship being done today, especially under the general rubric of the digital humanities, is specifically designed to leverage the unique attributes of networked data files and online interactive multimedia. Digital authoring and electronic scholarship thus point toward future models of library collection development and research support services that are still undergoing formative flux.

BACKGROUND AND OVERVIEW

While digital authoring has exploded since 2000, its academic roots date back to the introduction of personal computing in the mid-1980s; some would argue even earlier. Theorist Ted Nelson coined the term "hypertext" in 1965 and, in the 1980s, had begun circulating an early version of *Literary Machines* (Nelson, 1987), which influenced theorists like George Landow, Stuart Moulthrop, Jay David Bolter, and Michael Joyce. Michael Joyce, novelist and hypertext theorist, is credited with authoring the first true self-published hypertext novel, *Afternoon: A Story* (Joyce, 1990); and Bolter soon after authored one of the first academic books to examine and analyze this new digital genre (Bolter, 1991). Because mainstream publishers were expressing little interest in hypertext fiction at that time, Joyce and Bolter co-founded Eastgate Systems and collaborated to develop the first major software tool for hypertext self-publishing, Storyspace (Bolter, Joyce, Smith, & Eastgate Systems, 1993). Even as Storyspace was being introduced in academic writing and media labs on campuses such as Vassar College and Brown University, its lasting impact would largely be felt in the genres of self-published fiction and poetry. Digital authoring and self-publishing of nonfiction, especially for humanities computing projects, was more diffuse in the early days until Apple's development of HyperCard provided a high-profile platform for innovative digital scholarship such as the Blake Multimedia Project at California Polytechnic State University (Marx & Smith, 1994). HyperCard would be swiftly superseded, of course, by the tidal wave of change instigated by HTML and the emergence of the World Wide Web.

Although I never used Storyspace as an author, I had followed its development closely as I had known Michael Joyce since 1975–1976 when he taught at Jackson Community College (JCC) in Michigan at the time I was guest teaching a writing workshop there. By the 1980s, after I had left Michigan to work in public libraries in the Carolinas, the introduction of Apple's early personal computers, especially the revolutionary Macintosh, launched each of us independently into explorations of this new technology and its potential impacts on writing, learning, and libraries. Joyce established the Center for Narrative and Technology at JCC, served as a Visiting Fellow at the Yale University Artificial Intelligence Project (1984–1985), and then teamed with Jay David Bolter to develop Storyspace. Meanwhile, I was authoring early articles exploring potential impacts on libraries from both a theoretical perspective (Beagle, 1988) and a practical perspective (Beagle, 1989). I also taught an experimental writers' self-publishing workshop through Duke University's Office of Continuing Education where I drew upon a monologue/dialogue/discourse model proposed in the 1970s by psycholinguist Josephine Harris—a workshop I held not in a classroom, but in Duke's East Campus Library (the Lilly Library), where we experimented with an early Macintosh app for student creation, revision, and annotation of texts that I had developed myself in HyperCard.

After sharing my articles with Joyce, he introduced me to Bolter (J. Bolter, personal communication, May 9, 1991) and invited me to consult on a proposal for an Apple Library of Tomorrow Grant (ALOT) to create a new type of library-based writing/learning space for JCC. This initial ALOT proposal became a very early articulation of what would later come to be generally described throughout the library community as a "Learning Commons." It was not funded but paved the way for my successful 1995 ALOT grant for the Charleston Multimedia Project (CMP), a pioneering digital humanities project (Charleston County Library, 1996) that was featured in the book *Great American Websites* published by Osborne McGraw-Hill (Renehan, 1997). The CMP remained online and was actively being used as recently as early 2014. Its two-decade tenure online demonstrates the potential value of the library's playing the role of facilitator for digital self-publishing to benefit independent scholars. Such scholars, many of whom belong to the increasingly large population of seminomadic adjunct faculty, often feel marginalized from the colleges and universities where they teach and may lack access to departmental resources in support of their own scholarship. Libraries, academic and public, can help fill this void and give them access to platforms for digital authoring. A good example within CMP can be found in the online essay, "The Charleston Single House" (Beagle, 1995). This relatively brief essay examines various theories about the origin and development of an architectural style native and unique to the city of Charleston. While technically authored by me, it combines the theories and viewpoints of local independent scholars alongside those of mainstream architectural historians. The CMP was my own first foray into digital authoring and electronic scholarship and propelled me mid-career from public to academic libraries.

Even with the CMP successfully online, I still felt the need to establish my academic credentials by running the gauntlet of traditional publishing with two books, one through a trade press, the other academic. Both were successful—a point I make to stress that my own move to self-publishing is being driven by new opportunities, not old frustrations. My self-publishing projects thus far include a third book through print on demand and a fourth through Amazon's Kindle e-book channel, now properly known as Kindle Direct Publishing (KDP). I will briefly compare these four experiences, and—more importantly—describe why the different nature of each project dictated varying routes to publication. Then, I will offer thoughts about future scenarios.

The Charleston Single House

Acknowledgements

Photo: Single Houses on Ashley Ave.

From its settlement in 1670 until 1783, Charleston's development was almost entirely English, perhaps explaining why Charleston is not a "typical" Southern city, from either a social or architectural standpoint. From the simple austerity of the John Lining House, possibly pre-1700, to the Chippendale-influenced granduer of the Miles Brewton House c.1765, one can easily glimpse the strands of both social and architectural refinement.

In spite of the fact that Charleston's early architecture is highly English in flavor, there were certain local conditions that influenced its design. Most visitors are immediately fascinated by the numerous tall, slender houses with many-tiered piazzas--all seemingly too close for comfort.What they are seeing is the Charleston "Single House," which in fact is comfortable and habitable during hot and humid summers.

Colonial Charles Town actually saw a diverse array of architecture in keeping with the broad trans-atlantic English tradition of provincial ports and market towns, including row houses and large Georgian town houses. The Single House first appeared in the early 18th century, and gradually became the prevalent floor plan for the historic houses of antebellum Charleston. It proved remarkably adaptable in its own right. One sees very small Single Houses with plain facades directly fronting the street (as in 29 Archdale St. shown on left), as well as massive multi-level Single Houses with piazzas above the level of nearby trees (as shown in 45 East Bay St. below right).

Figure 5.1. Screen print of "The Charleston Single House," an online essay written by the author and posted as part of the Charleston Multimedia Project (1995). Created with the support of an Apple Library of Tomorrow Grant. Photographs by Donald Beagle.

TRADE PRESS: *THE INFORMATION COMMONS HANDBOOK* (ALA/NEAL-SCHUMAN, 2006)

This project grew out of articles I had written for the *Journal of Academic Librarianship*, published in the 1990s by JAI Press. Positive reaction prompted JAI to offer me a book contract in 1999. But print publishing was already churning, and the monograph division of JAI Press was soon swallowed by Ablex Publishing. Even as I revised the draft for Ablex, it was swallowed by a bigger fish named Elsevier, with yet another editorial slant. After further revisions, I found this an uncomfortable fit and withdrew. The project languished until 2004 when Neal-Schuman's editors saw growing momentum in support of the Information Commons (IC).

Publication through a trade press often involves incorporating (or responding to) reactions to the manuscript from one or more anonymous peer reviewers. In my case, two of the three peer reviewers were fortunately very favorable to both my book and the underlying IC concept. These two readers also offered constructive suggestions for improvement, which I rapidly incorporated. But the third reviewer was relentlessly hostile to the point of heaping sarcastic disdain on any notion that the Information Commons concept had any viable future in academic libraries. Fortunately for my book, the two favorable reviewers carried the day. But unfortunately, that single unfavorable reviewer forced me into a defensive posture of having to water down some of my more innovative and forward-looking content, including (ironically) my vision that the Information Commons was only the first stage of a developmental process that could lead to further enhancements such as a Learning Commons (LC), a pedagogical sandbox, and a Research Commons (RC), as a platform for digital authoring and electronic scholarship. The final published text was thus somewhat compromised and only mentioned these eventualities in a rather limited way. These anticipated developments have, of course, since proven to be resoundingly accurate over the years since 2006. Still, with contributions by colleagues D. Russell Bailey and Barbara Tierney, *The Information Commons Handbook* finally made its tortuous way to publication in October 2006.

Online media played a crucial role in the title's rapid acceptance. The book was announced on the INFOCOMMONS-L discussion list. More importantly, it was mentioned in Stephen Abram's high-profile blog. In a widely read blog at OCLC, Lorcan Dempsey described attending a workshop

Figure 5.2. Cover of *The Information Commons Handbook* (ALA/Neal-Schuman, 2006). Reproduced with permission.

where two experienced IC managers endorsed the book. Traditional media also played a key part: after receiving a "starred" review in *Library Journal*, the *Handbook* received positive reviews in seven professional journals worldwide. A WorldCat search now indicates that, of the 42 titles issued by Neal-Schuman in 2006, the *Handbook* currently ranks fourth in the number of catalogued library holdings. In 2014, the online posting of favorable Commons' assessments on campuses where the *Handbook* was used in IC development continues to drive sales. Google Scholar indicates the book has been cited 135 times—definitely an undercount—but still valid as a benchmark in comparison to Google Scholar counts for other monographs on the same topic.

This success has prompted numerous e-mail requests from faculty across the United States and around the world for a revised and updated second edition. While long anxious to proceed, I have no interest in taking the risk of exposing my work to any more hostile and uninformed peer readers whose influence might yet again compromise the quality of the *Handbook*'s content. In response to my request, ALA Publishing has therefore kindly transferred back to me all rights to future editions of *The Information Commons Handbook* (J. M. Jeffers, personal communication, April 3, 2013). With these rights in hand, I am now developing the revised and updated second edition to be published as an e-book with active links to online interactive multimedia resource files. Doing so will facilitate future Commons research and development across a wide spectrum of institutional environments in ways to best facilitate their use as platforms for innovative pedagogies. This edition will likely appear on Apple's iBook development platform as will be further discussed below.

ACADEMIC PRESS: *POET OF THE LOST CAUSE* (UNIVERSITY OF TENNESSEE PRESS, 2008)

While the *Handbook* met an emerging need, my second book addressed a long-standing gap in the scholarly record. Abram J. Ryan had been a battlefield chaplain in the Civil War, an important newspaper editor, and a poet, whose volume of verse became one of the best-selling collections in U.S. history since it went through 47 editions by the 1930s. Academics on numerous campuses had tried to write his biography but failed due to extraordinary difficulties researching Ryan's fragmented archival record. By the 1990s, Ryan was the most significant 19th-century U.S. poet without a biography.

In 2000, I discovered an important archive of Ryan papers, including wartime letters to his family from the battlefront. Further Ryaniana emerged via digitization projects such as READEX historical newspapers and Google Books. These proved critical not only in reconstructing Ryan's narrative, but also in documenting his cultural importance as a reason why his biography should be published. Ryan's fame during his lifetime (and for three decades after) was legendary. President McKinley recited his verses in the White House, for example; and Margaret Mitchell gave him a cameo role in *Gone with the Wind*. Today, his cultural impact has become occluded. With co-author Bryan Giemza, I unearthed findings that surprised historians: an interview from the *New York Times*; a poem in the *Saturday Evening Post*; praise by period critics in journals like *The Dial, New Eclectic*, and *Southern Literary Messenger*. Unlike the three peer readers who reviewed my trade press publication for Neal-Schuman, my manuscript submission to the University of Tennessee Press underwent extended examination and

Figure 5.3. Statue of the Civil War poet and Confederate chaplain Fr. Abram J. Ryan. The statue, still standing in Mobile, Alabama, was partly funded by a bequest from Joseph Pulitzer in recognition of Ryan's importance as a Southern newspaper editor during Reconstruction. This is one of a series of photographs by Donald Beagle. Another image of the statue from this series appeared as "Figure 29" in *Poet of the Lost Cause* (University of Tennessee Press, 2008).

FATHER RYAN

review by a full academic press editorial board. This was a highly demanding process that included one full rewrite; but it also resulted in a much-improved book that set the stage, I believe, for the highly favorable reviews it later received in nine scholarly journals.

Poet of the Lost Cause appeared in April 2008. Even though its topic seemed less amenable to digital publicity than the *Handbook*, online reactions were important. Professor Michael Pasquier, at Harvard on a fellowship from the American Academy of Arts and Letters, gave the book favorable comment in a highly regarded blog. On the popular side, newspapers that no longer included book reviews in their downsized paper editions gave it notice online. The scholarly print record was even more generous as the book received positive reviews in nine academic journals during a period when many deserving titles received only one or two reviews (if any). It was certainly not a best seller as it was issued into the fierce headwind of the 2008 economic collapse and subsequent budget cuts. But again, a World-Cat search indicates that of the 44 titles published in 2008 by University of Tennessee Press, *Poet of the Lost Cause* ranks sixth best in cataloged library holdings. And in 2014, it was chosen as a title for the highly selective "Essential Civil War Curriculum" compiled by the Virginia Center for Civil War Studies at Virginia Tech University (Hunter, 2014).

PRINT ON DEMAND: *THE LIFE AND ART OF RALPH RAY, JR.* (XLIBRIS, 2009)

Given these positive experiences, why turn to self-publishing? Print publishing entails financial risk to any institutional publisher. This risk weighs against acceptance of monographs that treat topics of regional or limited topical interest as in the following book on artist/illustrator Ralph Ray, Jr. This title also "illustrates" the cost factor of risk as publishers weigh expense versus likely demand. Any title requiring illustrations—color in particular— is at a significant disadvantage.

Ralph Ray, Jr. was an artistic prodigy who grew up during the 1930s in North Carolina and went on to become a successful illustrator of more than 50 young adult books issued by New York publishers through the 1950s. Ray also did remarkable watercolors of wildlife and illustrated two classic bird books in the 1940s for Oxford University Press (OUP) (Hall & Ray, 1946). In 2005, faculty colleague Robert Tompkins and I began roaming the southeast with a digital camera to document scattered originals in museums, galleries, and private collections. But the prospects for a biography remained dim. We felt the book might be a fit for OUP, but OUP expressed no interest. Fortunately, two foundations with ties to western North Carolina gave us production grants, which we used to underwrite self-publication through XLibris.

This book has been successful, but primarily through our own promotional efforts aimed at Ray's regional appeal. We gathered works from Ray's relatives for an exhibit at the Schiele Museum of Natural History, Gastonia, North Carolina, which included a well-attended reception and book signing. We submitted the book for scholarly recognition and received the Willie Parker Peace Award from the Society of North Carolina Historians. We underestimated, however, the demands of promotion on our own limited time and energy. Our efforts to reach libraries beyond the Carolinas had little success. For instance, my online search revealed a "Ralph Ray Jr. Collection" in the University of Minnesota's Children's

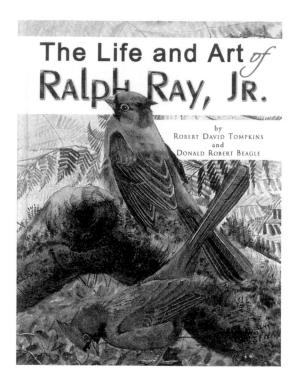

Figure 5.4. Cover image of *The Life and Art of Ralph Ray, Jr.* (XLibris, 2009). This self-published print-on-demand book was produced with the support of grants from the Carrie E. and Lena V. Glenn Foundation and the David Belk Cannon Foundation (original in color).

Literature Research Collections (CLRC), including original Ray sketches. But my e-mail to CLRC announcing our book brought no response, one of numerous cases where further follow-up seemed not worth the time and energy.

Neither Tompkins nor I were on Facebook in 2009. Were we to issue such a book now, we feel that Facebook could offer a promising channel. A number of authors I befriended in college writing seminars now use Facebook (and LinkedIn) to promote titles. Anne Serling, for example, linked her personal Facebook page to an auxiliary page promoting her newly released memoir about her father, screenwriter Rod Serling of *Twilight Zone* fame (Serling, 2013). As this is written, Facebook has announced the beta release of its new Graph Search app—a tool that, with future refinement, may offer users (and librarians) new ways to trace patterns of "likes" and endorsements across the social network. Were a similar app designed for the academic blogosphere, with appropriate metadata, we might have a tool to make visible what used to be nicknamed the "invisible college" with associated article and book recommendations (Beagle, 1999).

KINDLE E-BOOK: *THE OUTSIDER ART OF MEREDITH JOY MERRITT* (KDP, 2014)

While Ralph Ray had become a neglected and largely forgotten artist by 2009 (at least beyond his native town of Gastonia, North Carolina), his work had been mainstream in concept and content and thus successful and recognized at least during his lifetime. But scholars and critics have become increasingly aware of a varied group of visual artists whose work has been marginalized from the start because it has failed to fit comfortably into mainstream commercial or academic genres. The work of such artists has been given the general label "outsider art," which signifies art that either remains deeply rooted in folk traditions (such as the work of Grandma Moses) or uses unorthodox and innovative media and techniques that mainstream gallery owners and museum curators have difficulties incorporating into exhibitions and sometimes do not recognize as having intrinsic aesthetic value. In one important sense, such outsider artists experience a marginalization comparable to that experienced by adjunct faculty and independent scholars.

I discovered such an outsider artist in my own explorations of the native art scene in the gallery crawls periodically held in Charlotte's celebrated "NoDa" arts district. Meredith Joy Merritt was a faculty member at the University of North Carolina–Charlotte, who had become intensely drawn to visual arts as an expressive medium even though her academic training and career had formally taken a different direction. Her vision and creative works were unorthodox from the start, although clearly influenced by recognized artists such as Jackson Pollock and Mark Rothko. Even as she was beginning to find an audience in a number of NoDa district galleries, Merritt began experiencing neuromuscular symptoms of what would soon be diagnosed as multiple sclerosis (MS). As the MS increasingly degraded her ability to do finely controlled brushwork over the following years, Merritt battled back by adopting new media, such as collage and 3-D assemblages, and by developing a highly individualized technique of "flung pigment" using nail polish on sandpaper. Because I found that her art was quietly attracting the attention and respect of serious local art critics and academics, I decided to document her accumulated body of work with my digital camera, even as her MS was gradually bringing her creative endeavors to a halt. Eventually she left her faculty position at UNC–Charlotte to go on disability leave. My decision to self-publish a photographic record of Merritt's body of work using Amazon's e-book channel of Kindle Direct Publishing (KDP) was very much influenced by the artist's personal preferences. She wanted to make her work visible and available as inexpensively as possible to a wide swath of fellow artists, extended family, and former colleagues. This resulted in the June 2014 release of my KDP title, *The Outsider Art of Meredith Joy Merritt*.

My work on this e-book has revealed that, while KDP now offers perhaps the most high-profile and easily accessed channel for digital self-publishing available today, it is not a channel well suited to serious academic scholarship in general or to image-intensive publications in particular. KDP offers a platform optimized for simple narrative text, most often uploaded by way of direct conversion from original documents in Microsoft Word. Amazon's conversion utility works reasonably well for such basic flowing text but is rife with unexpected formatting pitfalls for large image collections. Such simple format actions as hard returns and page break inserts in MS Word originals cause ripple effects in uploaded KDP files that result in a self-published e-book displaying itself very differently through the various free apps Amazon

Figure 5.5. An image selected from *The Outsider Art of Meredith Joy Merritt* (Kindle Direct Publishing, 2014). Title: *Early or Late?* (medium: collage). Photograph by Donald Beagle (original in color).

has devised for e-book distribution beyond its own Kindle e-reader tablets. This includes its apps for Windows, IOS, and Android operating systems.

My KDP e-book of Merritt's art, as a result, displays very well on a Kindle Fire color tablet with one image per screen. The images are somewhat small, but color rendition and resolution are excellent. When the same file is accessed through Amazon's Kindle app for Windows on a laptop, by contrast, the images are larger (which is good); but blank screens appear between many of the images that cause readers to wonder whether images might be missing (none are actually missing). And when the same published file is displayed though an IOS device, such as my iPhone 6 or iPad 2, some sections of the book have blank screens between images while other sections display two images per screen. These results are especially disappointing given that the KDP upload utility includes a "preview" function that supposedly emulates the final format and appearance of any e-book contents in the context of these respective apps before publication is finalized. My e-book previewed perfectly in this visual preview emulation phase in each app emulation, showing one large image per screen with no blank screens. This proved to be highly misleading when applied to the final result over multiple platforms. For these reasons, I plan no further self-publishing through KDP and will be focusing my own future digital scholarship self-publishing though Apple's iBook development software.

APPLE IBOOK IN PROGRESS:
THE LIFE AND COLLECTED WORKS OF FR. ABRAM J. RYAN

Research on the Ryan biography uncovered a remarkable number of poems and essays never before published or published in fugitive outlets. These are extremely important but did not fit into the biography. When I received a formal invitation to deliver a presentation in Richmond for the Civil War Sesquicentennial, I felt my topic ("Fr. Abram Ryan and the Civil War Chaplains") would make late 2015 an ideal time to release a major new collection of Ryan's writings, along with a biographical supplement to incorporate research discoveries made since 2008. While the University of Tennessee Press has been wonderful in supporting the 2008 biography, I have decided to pursue this as an Apple iBook. This gives me production flexibility, along with the capacity for interactive multimedia that can be creatively used to at last convey the full scale and scope of Ryan's extraordinary 19th-century cultural impact.

The Ryan iBook project, in other words, will demonstrate the "flip side" of the motivation to pursue digital self-publishing. Instead of providing a publishing venue of last resort for works that lack alternate mainstream outlets, Apple's iBook platform is designed to help even widely published academic authors create *enhanced* works of scholarship that engage readers in visual, auditory, and networked multimedia dimensions quite beyond the expressive capabilities of traditional print publishing. Scholar Jacob L. Wright recently described his own enhanced iBook project (on King David) as

> ... a game changer. Now we can much more easily disseminate our work in art history, archaeology, and many other scholarly fields that have presented high hurdles to print publishing. A fully enhanced e-book can do the work of two or more traditional print volumes: Authors can address the general reading public and lower-level students in the main body of the text, while treating technical matters for advanced readers in more detail by providing electronic links to extensive pullout or pop-up windows. (Wright, 2014)

Readers can also click on icons to pull up supplementary material, primary sources, photographs, maps, video clips, animations, and publishers' Web sites. Wright's enhanced e-book is, however, not an exercise in purely defined self-publishing as it was undertaken in conjunction with Cambridge University Press.

CONCLUSION: FUTURE STRATEGIES

As librarians, we need to track developments across a number of social media fronts beyond established channels like Pinterest and Goodreads: future refinements to Google Analytics and Alerts, Facebook's aforementioned Graph Search app, and federated knowledge discovery keyed to what Lederman terms the "deep web" (Lederman, 2009). What might librarians do with access to reader analytics as discussed in the *Wall Street Journal* article "Your E-Book Is Reading You" (Alter, 2012)? Crowd-source collection development? For now, the low-hanging fruit, in my view, is still in the blogosphere. My first two books clearly benefited from its impact. As a librarian, I am consequently more attuned to seeking influential blogs in disciplines where I might find mention of authors and titles. Blogging has clearly become a typical first rung on the self-publishing ladder. Dissertation research by Carolyn Hank supports digital curation of academic blogs and reveals that 80% of scholar bloggers believe their blogs should be preserved for future access (Hank, 2011). The best deserve to be archived for their own worth, perhaps using a curatorial tool like BlogForever (BlogForever, 2013). Tracking disciplinary aggregators like Researchblogging.org can yield blogged references to articles and monographs. For instance, a study posted at altmetrics.org explores preferences among science bloggers for articles in certain subcategories of journals (Shema & Bar-Ilan, 2011). By early 2016, I will definitely be seeking opportunities to post mention of my Apple iBook within Civil War–related academic and popular blogs.

On the public library front, on June 24, 2014, *Library Journal (LJ)* and BiblioBoard announced the launch of beta versions of the *LJ* SELF-e platform and curation service at public library systems in Los Angeles, San Diego, Cuyahoga County (Ohio), the Arizona State Library, and through the statewide Massachusetts eBook Project. *LJ*'s SELF-e connects self-published authors with public libraries and their patrons. Through the SELF-e submission portal,

> . . . authors in the beta libraries' communities can submit their self-published eBook(s) for display and patron access across that state. Additionally, they have the opportunity to opt-in to allow *LJ* to evaluate and select titles for inclusion in curated genre collections that participating public libraries will make available to their patrons all over the United States. SELF-e submissions will be accepted on a rolling basis, with the first collections set to be released later this year. . . . SELF-e, a royalty-free service, appeals to writers looking for the next-generation discovery service for [self-published] eBooks in libraries. (Books News Desk, 2014)

On the academic front, while both open-access e-journals and self-archived institutional repositories are proliferating, we are likely to see scholarly self-publishing become respectable more rapidly within management frameworks that incorporate some process of preview opportunity for scholarly examination even in advance of formal peer review. The classic example, of course, is the preprint server arXiv, where mathematicians, physicists, and computer scientists have uploaded over a million academic papers since 1991. Those academic libraries that do decide to adopt an active role as publishers of digital journals and/or monographs would be well advised to incorporate some of the functional lessons of arXiv, while also seeking opportunities for cross-institutional collaboration.

REFERENCES

Alter, A. (2012). Your e-book is reading you. *Wall Street Journal*, July 19, 2012. Retrieved from http://online.wsj.com/article/SB100014240527023048703045774909500514383o4.html

Beagle, D. (1988). Libraries and the implicate order: A contextual approach to theory. *Libri: International Library Review, 38, 26–44.*

Beagle, D. (1989). Online with a Macintosh. *OCLC Microcomputing, 6, 13–26.*

Beagle, D. (1995). *The Charleston single house. Charleston Multimedia Project.* Retrieved from http://www.ccpl.org/content.asp?id=15762&action=detail&catID=6044&parentID=5748

Beagle, D. (1999). Visualization of metadata. *Information Technology and Libraries, 18, 192–199.*

BlogForever Consortium. (2013). *BlogForever* [Computer software]. Retrieved from http://blogforever.eu/

Bolter, J. D. (1991). *Writing space: The computer, hypertext, and the history of writing.* Hillsdale, NJ: L. Erlbaum Associates.

Bolter, J. D., Joyce, M., Smith, J. B., & Eastgate Systems. (1993). *Storyspace* [Computer software]. Cambridge, MA: Eastgate Systems.

Books News Desk. (2014). Library Journal and BiblioBoard announce the launch of beta versions of the LJ SELF-e. *Booksworld.com.* Retrieved from http://www.broadwayworld.com/bwwbooks/article/Library-Journal-and-BiblioBoard-Announce-the-Launch-of-Beta-Versions-of-the-LJ-SELF-e-20140624?PageSpeed=noscript#

Charleston County Library. (1996). *The Charleston multimedia project.* Charleston, SC: Charleston County Library. Retrieved from Internet Archive at https://web.archive.org/web/20101213055052/http://ccpl.org/content.asp?name=Site&catID=5747&parentID=5372 Note: for a discussion of how the CMP relates to both digital humanities and the development of the "Commons model" in academic libraries, see my three-part guest blog for ACRL: Beagle, D. Digital humanities in the research commons: Precedents & prospects. (2014,

January 30). Association of College & Research Libraries/ dh+lib. Retrieved from http://acrl.ala.org/dh/2014/01/30/digital-humanities-in-the-research -commons-precedents-prospects-3/

Hall, H. M., & Ray, R. (1946). *The ruffed grouse.* New York: Oxford University Press.

Hall, H. M., & Ray, R. (1946). *Woodcock ways.* New York: Oxford University Press.

Hank, C. (2011). *Scholars and their blogs: Characteristics, preferences, and perceptions impacting digital preservation* (Doctoral dissertation). Carolina Digital Repository. Chapel Hill, NC: University of North Carolina. Retrieved from https://cdr.lib.unc.edu/indexablecontent/uuid:4a2c4438 -2c34-460f-a377-f253365324f9

Hunter, L., & Virginia Center for Civil War Studies. (2014). The lost cause. *Essential Civil War Curriculum.* Blacksburg, VA: Virginia Tech University. Retrieved from http://www.essential.civilwar.vt.edu/1536.html

Joyce, M. (1990). *Afternoon: A story* [Hypertext novel]. Watertown, MA: Eastgate Systems.

Lederman, A. (2009). Science research: Journey to ten thousand sources. *Special Libraries Association Annual Conference.* Retrieved from http://www.sla .org/pdfs/sla2009/SciResJourneyTenThouSources.pdf

Marx, S., & Smith, D. (1994). The Blake multimedia project. San Luis Obispo, CA: California Polytechnic State University. Retrieved from http://cla.calpoly.edu /~smarx/Blake/blakeproject.html

Nelson, T. H. (1987). *Literary machines: The report on, and of, Project Xanadu concerning word processing, electronic publishing, hypertext, thinkertoys, tomorrow's intellectual revolution, and certain other topics including knowledge, education and freedom.* Swarthmore, PA: Theodor H. Nelson.

Renehan, E. (1997). *Great American websites: An online discovery of a hidden America.* Berkeley: Osborne McGraw-Hill.

Serling, A. (2013). *As I knew him: My dad, Rod Serling.* New York, NY: Citadel Press/Kensington Publishing.

Shema, H., & Bar-Illan, J. (2011). Characteristics of Researchblogging.org science blogs and bloggers, altmetrics.org. Retrieved from http://altmetrics.org /workshop2011/shema-vo/

Wright, J. L. (2014). What enhanced e-books can do for scholarly authors. *The Digital Campus: A Newsletter of the Chronicle of Higher Education.* Retrieved from http://chronicle.com/article/What-Enhanced-E-Books-Can-Do/145969/

6 | Book Vendors and Self-Publishing

Bob Nardini, ProQuest Books

"Libraries do a lousy job of collecting self-published works," wrote Brian Kenney, *Publishers Weekly* columnist and director of New York's White Plains Public Library. This confession is one sign among many that libraries now want to do better. One reason for the "lousy job" may be that the job itself is lousy, as White Plains learned when the library's new policy of "you ask, we buy" yielded a surprising number of requests for self-published books, especially young adult (YA) fiction. "Setting this up," reported the library's manager of technical services and collection development, "researching requests, contacting patrons, ordering from vendors outside our usual stream, and processing in-house is time consuming" (Kenney, 2013, p. 19).

Book vendors do several things for libraries. First, and most basically, when a library submits an order, a vendor will try to locate and obtain the book, then bill and ship it to the library. Next, vendors normally offer services to help libraries identify and select books of likely interest by creating lists, generating new title notifications, and operating approval plans and standing order programs. Then, vendors maintain bibliographic databases and online systems to enable searching, ordering, and other functions. Finally, vendors offer cataloging and physical processing services for the books libraries acquire.

While over the past decade the rise first of e-books and then of patron- or demand-driven acquisitions programs have added complexity, these traditional functions remain at the center of what book vendors do. Now another movement is on the rise, one that has already disrupted other parts of the book trade. How much help, at White Plains or anywhere else where library attitudes have turned, can book vendors provide? How well do traditional library book vendor services lend themselves to self-publishing, or "indie publishing," as the phenomenon has come to be known?

TRADITIONAL VENDOR SERVICES

Sometimes, reasonably well. From a vendor's point of view, locating and obtaining a self-published print book can be easier than doing that for many of the more obscure campus- or society-based scholarly books that academic vendors, at least, if not public library vendors used to covering a narrower range of the publishing world, have always provided to libraries. This sort of book resembles self-publishing in any case, publishing so truly mission-driven and independent that the idea of having "customers" who might want orders filled was sometimes a distraction. Literary small press publishing is much the same. Minus anything like the consolidation of today's self-publishing landscape into a handful of large author-oriented companies (Bowker, 2014), vendor experience with this type of book makes library orders for many self-published books seem like easy work.

Not, however, work entirely without complexities. Most derive from the same consolidation that in other ways has simplified the business. Baker & Taylor (B&T) and Ingram are the two largest North American library book vendors. But it's far from the case that either one is strictly a library vendor. In Ingram's case, the print-on-demand (POD) company Lightning Source and self-publishing platform IngramSpark are two components of the larger Ingram Content Group. Ingram Library Services is another component of the group. In the case of Baker & Taylor, the 2013 purchase of Bookmasters by B&T's parent company, the private equity firm Castle Harlan, gave B&T a sister company with POD and author services capabilities (Schwartz, 2013). Amazon, whose CreateSpace is a leading author services company, is in a number of ways across the retail and library book business a competitor as well as a business partner with both B&T and Ingram. Since these and other author services companies offer their authors a choice of distribution packages and since the author services companies themselves make various POD and distribution arrangements with other companies, the willingness or even the ability of B&T

and Ingram to fill a firm order for a self-published print book originating with a company that might be a direct or indirect competitor can make for an intricate equation.

A vendor's ability to fill a library's firm order will largely depend on the scope of its title database. The major North American vendor databases are B&T's Title Source 3, its academic subsidiary YBP's GOBI, Ingram's ipage, and for Ingram's academic library customers, OASIS. These title databases are all built in different ways through unique combinations of external bibliographic loads from publishers and from agencies such as the Library of Congress or Nielsen as well as from incoming customer orders. Shared internal systems may also contribute, such as those at Ingram hosting IngramSpark titles and also feeding metadata to ipage and OASIS. At B&T, Title Source 3 and GOBI would at least potentially have access to titles from Bookmasters. The chances of a librarian finding a given self-published title in these respective databases would depend in part, again, upon corporate relationships having little to do with the library market.

Since the goal of nearly every self-publishing author is to have his or her books available for sale there, the database of record for self-publishing, however, is without question Amazon. Library sales, if in mind at all, would be a secondary concern for most authors. Even companies competing with CreateSpace for authors have no choice about sending title metadata to Amazon, whose title universe, print books aside, might well be the only place to find a self-published e-book. Even if a vendor title database did include a self-published title, a library seeking to buy the book might not look there, only because they are used to turning to Amazon. For library vendors, there would be little point in attempting to match Amazon in the scope of their database for self-published books.

Despite all this, libraries do place successful firm orders for self-published books with vendors. A 2012 study of a larger sample showed that vendors had attached their holding symbol to 95 of 114 titles found in OCLC, likely indicating orders filled by those vendors. In 18 instances, original records had been contributed by either B&T, by B&T's subsidiary YBP, or by Ingram (Bradley, Fulton, & Helm, 2012). Vendors charge libraries different rates for different levels of cataloging, and libraries contract for what they judge they need and can afford. When a self-published book requires original cataloging, rather than manipulation of a record that already exists, the extra work should be covered by the higher price contracting libraries pay for that level of service. Otherwise, for vendors there is nothing beyond normal in cataloging a self-published book obtained on behalf of a library placing an order.

WHOLE FOODS?

The keynote address at a 2013 Charleston Conference preconference about self-publishing was delivered by Mark Sandler, director of the Center for Library Initiatives (CLI), Committee on Institutional Cooperation (CIC), who made an analogy between grocery stores and libraries (SelfPub 2.0, 2013). With traditional chain grocery stores—Kroger was his example— well-known national brands validate the worth of the store, which simply provides shelf space for Campbell's, for Del Monte, and the rest. At Whole Foods, on the other hand, the store validates the brands and even the products, which may be unfamiliar to many shoppers. In libraries, the "brands" stocked on the shelves usually are books from better known publishers. Why couldn't libraries be more like Whole Foods and provide validation for quality with the library "brand"?

Of course this would require some kind of evaluation process. As the Whole Foods Market Web site says, "We don't sell just anything. The products we sell must meet our rigorous standards. . . . We carefully evaluate each and every product we sell" (Whole Foods Market, 2014). How rigorous should a library's standards be for self-published books? How carefully should a library examine every product added to its shelves? Clearly, some degree of filtering on Bowker's 450,000+ annual total (Bowker, 2014) would seem to be needed. Could vendors help? The current vendor infrastructure produces ongoing recommendations for all sorts of other books, from romance novels to scientific conferences and beyond. Why not self-published YA novels, or mysteries, or local histories, or anything else?

For vendors, there would be two questions. First, how do they find titles worth recommending? And second, would enough new business be gained to justify the work?

Today, a good deal of vetting has already taken place on any vendor book announcements or recommendations reaching a library. Much of the vetting, however, has been on the part of a publisher, not the vendor, since publisher acquisitions processes substantially narrow things down at the very outset. In fact, editorial selectivity by publishers is commonly cited in the success stories about self-published authors, which themselves have become almost a genre. "Nobody was willing to take a chance," said author Darcie Chan to a *Wall Street Journal* reporter, for example. "It was too much of a publishing risk." Chan was talking about her debut novel, *The Mill River Recluse*, a book turned down by a dozen publishers and 100 literary agents before she chose to self-publish, which then reached national best-seller lists with sales of more than 400,000 e-books (Alter, 2011).

Chan took advantage of marketing services available to self-published authors. If she had published traditionally, her publisher would have provided some level of marketing support, which is the next vetting function publishers perform, after title acquisition. Vendor operations are organized to focus on the most basic level of this support, which is the new title metadata publishers routinely push out in a host of ways. ONIX data feeds, printed and online catalogs, Excel files, Advance Book Information sheets, personal presentations—in these and other ways publishers organize and disseminate the bibliographic and pricing information vendors need to populate their databases and run the selection and recommendation services they direct toward libraries. Beyond basic metadata, publishers will orchestrate some measure of publicity for more promising titles; for titles they judge less promising, little or none. Vendors take note, and stock inventories accordingly.

With self-published titles, this entire publisher-to-vendor-to-library marketing infrastructure is missing. Nobody is pushing out structured marketing information to vendors, who, in order to notify libraries about the best self-published titles, would first need to find them. Vendors would need to develop new routines to monitor Web sites and blogs and to constantly find new ones, to follow certain review sources, to keep up with Twitter and Facebook and Pinterest, perhaps to develop relationships with authors and author groups. Many of the titles they might find would lack basic bibliographic detail, not infrequently even an ISBN, let alone the more elaborate metadata a traditional publisher would provide (Bradley et al., 2012). All of this makes self-published titles more difficult to identify, evaluate, and process than books from traditional publishers.

ONE VENDOR'S EXPERIENCE

"More difficult" means, of course, "more expensive." But it does not mean "impossible." Since the work wouldn't be routine, it would be more costly for a vendor to offer self-published books to libraries than to offer other books. What would a vendor's reward be in attempting to provide traditional services for these nontraditional books?

Ingram Coutts, the academic division of Ingram, has made a modest effort toward doing this. The company has many libraries among its customers in Canada, where self-publishing has been within the vision of academic libraries for years. Book publishing takes place in most parts of the country, even with a population of only 35 million people settled unevenly across a vast geography. Many of these Canadian books would not be published or recognized at all, however, without the support of grants and prizes for publishers and writers offered by federal and provincial governments, who consider the support of Canadian culture a mandate (Book and Periodical Council, 2015). The publishing that results from this combination of population, geography, and patronage is often conducted on a small scale, sometimes by individuals.

Original People, Original Television: The Launching of the Aboriginal Peoples Television Network is a good example (David, 2012). This book tells the story of how broadcasters distributing community-based television programming across northern Canada, mostly from Aboriginal and Inuit producers, came together in 1999 to form the Aboriginal Peoples Television Network, today a national enterprise based in Winnipeg, Manitoba. The author, Jennifer David, a member of the Cree Nation, took part in these early efforts (David, 2015). Her book was the one and only title ever from its "publisher," Debwe Communications, David's own Ottawa-based communications consulting company.[1]

OCLC's WorldCat database shows 15 holdings for the book.[2] Ten are in Canada, including one public library, one provincial legislative library, Library and Archives Canada, and seven universities. Three American universities reported holdings to OCLC as did the Library of Congress. On the other side of the world, in New Zealand, the University of Auckland also reported its holding. Since many library holdings for self-published books never find their way into WorldCat (Dilevko & Dali, 2006), these 15 records underrepresent the record of *Original People,*

Original Television. In fact, Ingram Coutts sold copies to 21 libraries. These sales accounted for most of the WorldCat listings. The other library customers ranged from the London School of Economics and Political Science, to the University of Saskatchewan, to Thompson Rivers University of Kamloops, British Columbia.

Jennifer David had a good topic and by all signs wrote a good book, one that will provide unique value in the collections of libraries acquiring it. For Ingram Coutts, 21 sales was not a bad total. A prepublication record for *Original People, Original Television* was loaded into the company's database in 2011 through a bibliographic feed staff monitored from Library and Archives Canada (LAC). The author's book launch was in September 2012. In January 2013, when Ingram Coutts obtained a copy, staff updated the book's database record. Most of the 21 sales came from bibliographic announcements from a process matching the updated bibliographic record against library subject "profiles" established with Ingram Coutts.[3] These matches produced more than 80 notifications to library selectors, which were displayed on the OASIS customer interface. The last library order to date for the book reached Ingram Coutts in July 2014, one of two orders received that year; all the rest were submitted by July 2013.

How representative of self-published titles was *Original People, Original Television*? A study of Ingram Coutts' activity for the 12 months from August 2013 to July 2014 shows that it was not typical.[4] During that year, the company offered 380 self-published titles to customers in the same way *Original People, Original Television* had been offered. Most were Canadian titles selected from LAC records and other sources. Thirty-three titles, however, were published in the United States, most of them identified from favorable reviews in the "PW Select" section of *Publishers Weekly*.

Only four titles sold more than 10 copies. All four were Canadian, led by another title on Aboriginal studies, *Balancing Two Worlds: Jean-Baptiste Assiginack and the Odawa Nation, 1768–1866*, published in Saskatoon, Saskatchewan, which sold 18 copies. Following that were a study of the Canadian War of 1812 heroine Laura Secord, published in the town where she lived, Niagara-on-the-Lake, Ontario, which sold 13 copies; a history of the Allied Bomber Command in World War II, published in Thunder Bay, Ontario, which sold 12; and a biography of a Cree warrior and shaman, published in Calgary, Alberta, which sold 11.

The company's sales for everything else amounted to fewer than 10 copies per title. Twenty-seven titles sold between five and nine copies, 161 sold between two and four copies, 108 sold one copy, and 80 did not sell at all. The best-selling American title was *Hidden in Plain Sight: The Other People in Norman Rockwell's America*, a book about "the stories of the Asian, African, and Native Americans who modeled for Norman Rockwell. These people of color, though often hidden in plain sight, are present throughout Rockwell's more than 4000 illustrations" (Petrick, 2015). Rockwell, the painter whose work was long considered the embodiment of kitsch, is today enjoying a turnaround evident in museum acquisitions and exhibitions, auction sales, a widely reviewed 2013 biography published by Farrar, Straus and Giroux, and articles such as one in the *New York Times* that took note of his "major . . . reappraisal" (Stewart, 2014). So like Jennifer David, the author Jane Allen Petrick had a good topic. She also, like David, published the book under the imprint of a consulting company, Informed Decisions Publishing. Unlike David, though, her book does not appear in WorldCat at all; and Ingram Coutts' academic customers did not show much interest with just three orders. One yardstick for the book's record is an earlier book written by Petrick (Schiesel, 1973), a biography of Otis Redding, published by Doubleday, with 217 WorldCat holdings.

ONE TITLE'S EXPERIENCE

Another self-published title offered to Ingram Coutts' customers in 2014 was *Quack This Way* by Bryan A. Garner (2013). While the title is peculiar, its subtitle clarifies what the book is about: *David Foster Wallace & Bryan A. Garner Talk Language and Writing*. Wallace, the late novelist "widely considered one of the most brilliant writers of his generation" (Gregoire, 2014), became friends with Garner through a 2001 review Wallace wrote for *Harper's* of Garner's *Dictionary of Modern American Usage*. In 2006 Garner interviewed Wallace and in 2013 published the interview in this book, overcoming a "mental block" that had prevented him from doing so after Wallace's 2008 suicide (Garner, 2013, p. 19). *Quack This Way* is full of opinions elicited by Garner from Wallace in a voice that many devoted readers would recognize and relish. Here Wallace laments that a passion he and Garner shared was not widely shared by others:

> And people like you and me, we just don't have our finger on the
> pulse anymore. What people are looking for is not the kind of
> stuff we're talking about. You'll want to cut this out. I don't say
> that to my students because my line with them is still, "Look,
> you're at this elite school, you're going to end up in the profes-
> sions. . . . Right? You need to quack this way." Forget all this stuff
> about it being beautiful and having centuries of tradition and
> being the adventure of a lifetime. But the truth is that between
> sophisticated advertising and national level politics, I am at a loss
> as to what people's use of language is now meant to convey and
> connote to the receiver. It's so different from the way I myself am
> wired that I just don't get it. (Garner, 2013, pp. 110–111)

Quack This Way was noticed in *The New Yorker* (Max, 2013), among other
places. Goodreads has 198 ratings and 44 reviews, most very positive. Wallace's best known novel, *Infinite Jest*, has 1,905 OCLC WorldCat holdings.
The first Wallace biography, published by Viking (Max, 2012), shows 1,140
holdings. Garner's own most recent book, the 2014 10th edition of *Black's
Law Dictionary*, which he has edited since 1999, has 4,488. *Quack This
Way*, by contrast, has 32 holding libraries, many of them at law schools.[5]
For Ingram Coutts, notifications in July 2014 to 56 academic library selectors have yielded, to date, four orders. Two originated overseas, one from
the University of Liverpool, one from the Zentralbibliothek Zürich. American libraries generated the other two orders, one from the University of
Virginia, one from the University of St. Thomas, St. Paul, Minnesota.

With his own long record as an author, Garner was not in need of
another formally published book (About Bryan A. Garner, 2012). Ingram's
academic library staff learned of the book from IngramSpark, where Garner
had chosen to publish it. *Quack This Way* is a small book, 137 pages long,
with a nicely designed cover featuring a caricature of Wallace, an index, and
a touching 21-page introduction written by Garner to frame the interview.
To date, *Quack This Way* has altogether sold about a thousand copies.

Why the disconnect between *Quack This Way* and libraries? At public
libraries, surely some of the many readers who enjoyed *Infinite Jest* and
other Wallace books would have been delighted to find *Quack This Way*
on their local new book shelf; but only nine public libraries show WorldCat

holdings. At colleges and universities, Wallace's body of work will without a doubt be the focus of seminars, theses, and dissertations for years to come.[6] The book would seem to have a waiting readership, of modest size at least, at both types of libraries.

Quack This Way simply fell outside normal selection routines at public libraries. It was not reviewed in *Library Journal, Publishers Weekly, Kirkus,* or *Booklist,* the places a traditional publisher would have worked toward securing reviews.[7] The *New Yorker* notice was a "Web-only" publication not printed in the magazine. The many other online notices in Goodreads and elsewhere must, for the most part, have been beyond the orbit of public library selectors; Ingram did not place the book on its public library selection lists; and that any other vendor would have is not likely. Many academic librarians, oriented in recent years toward patron-driven acquisitions programs, have become reluctant to select books even from mainstream publishers (Nixon, Freeman, & Ward, 2014; Swords, 2011). In the field of English, where narrow monographs are all but a stock example of books with a good chance of seldom being read and never borrowed, selectors are possibly more defensive than in many other areas.

WHAT SHOULD VENDORS DO?

With the 32 WorldCat exceptions, interested readers were left to themselves to find *Quack This Way.* Which, by the evidence, many did. Should vendors see helping connect libraries with self-published books as an opportunity?

The first library to make great numbers of self-published e-books available to patrons in a highly visible way was Colorado's Douglas County Libraries (DCL) where the vision of director Jamie LaRue was motivated in part by a wish to shrink as much as he could the role of vendors in library e-book acquisitions. "The vendors were screwing us," as he put it to a reporter in describing the digital warehousing and contracting system built at Douglas County where inexpensive books from self-publishing authors, free of user restrictions, became a centerpiece of the library's mission. LaRue's vision caught on to the point of acronym as other library systems around the country are trying their own versions of the "DCL model" (Scott, 2013).

How far LaRue and others will be able to go in shrinking their dependence on commercial e-book vendors is an open question. But most of the "gold rush" (Herther, 2013) in self-publishing that has attracted so much media attention has occurred with e-books, and this is where most vendor activity has taken place so far. In 2014, OverDrive, the market leader in providing e-books to public libraries, began to offer self-published books from Smashwords, a leading platform for e-book publishing and distribution, matching an earlier move by B&T (Enis, 2014). In another collaboration launched in 2014, BiblioBoard and *Library Journal* provided authors an option on their SELF-e platform to allow *LJ* to evaluate books for possible inclusion in curated collections available to participating public libraries ("Cuyahoga County," 2014), a service combining distribution and evaluation. Mark Coker, who founded Smashwords, described his company's efforts at vetting titles in order to select a relatively small percentage of them for public library collections as "a lot more complicated for us than we expected" (Hadro, 2013). Smashwords used an algorithm based at least in part on author output and sales, resulting in an evaluation process with a high degree of automation, probably necessary for any process attempting to organize any substantial part of today's enormous universe of self-published e-books.

Whatever their differences in process, vendor-assembled collections will often be the end result for public libraries. While vendors like Smashwords do enable title-by-title sales, any library wishing to scale up its patron offerings would find this a long, hard road; and a road longer and harder still for those libraries applying a degree of their own vetting process at the title level. Even when reviews happen to be available, "we're often left in the tough spot of reviewing the review source," as a librarian at the Free Library of Philadelphia put it, referring to what might be the doubtful authority of author-paid reviews or reader reviews (Hadro, 2013). For vendors, the low price of self-published e-books would be another issue. If for authors the price point of 99¢ is "no longer the path to riches" with the current "pricing sweet spots" for e-books now at $2.99 and $3.99 (Sargent, 2014), library vendors would find thin margins in title-level transactions even in this higher range. Library demands are far greater than the demands of individual readers who go online to buy themselves a novel. For vendors having to meet those demands, prices like these would mean a difficult path to profits.

It's doubtful libraries would willingly pay a multiple of list price, even for low prices such as these, which is what vendors would require in order to match their margins on traditional books. For vendors, another consideration would be that sales per copy for most self-published books would likely be lower than for traditional books. This would be a negative equation, since in order to sell the same number of copies, a vendor would require less labor for traditional books, as the number of different titles needing to be processed would be lower. Perhaps, instead of different title-level pricing, an alternative approach might be an annual fee for providing the service of covering self-published books.

Self-published books in print format would be another open question as there is nothing about print that lends itself to collections or other forms of mass acquisition or anything else that would yield economies for vendors or for libraries. Nor is there evidence of mass demand from library patrons. The demand public libraries do more often see comes from authors, sometimes happy to donate a free copy, who would like to see their book in a local library. Of course these free copies are hardly free to the libraries that would need to evaluate, process, and maintain them. "Please do not send a sample of your book," requests the Toronto Public Library, for example, on its Web site page directed at self-published authors. "If the selector wants to see it, we will buy a copy" (Toronto Public Library, 2015). When libraries do decide to buy a self-published print book, the purchase can be mainstreamed if their vendor's database is up to the task as already discussed. Otherwise, libraries buying directly from authors or placing one-off orders on Amazon or another site will bear high staff costs for these one-off transactions, costs not likely offset by the generally lower prices of self-published books.

Academic libraries present another open question for the vendors who serve them. Public libraries and their vendors can see evidence of demand for self-published e-books merely by looking at the latest best-seller list. In the academic world, best-sellers are rare and even those books that do sell relatively well would be dwarfed in sales by many self-published books read by general readers. Usually academic authors publish for reasons other than sales; and, while some academic authors have done well publishing on their own, the same "gold rush" pursued by popular authors seems an unlikely prospect in the scholarly world (Bosquet, 2013).

For vendors, the implication would be not to expect strong sales for those self-published books they might offer to academic libraries, a view confirmed by a study of OCLC holdings that found academic libraries "not as receptive to self-publishers as public libraries" (Dilevko & Dali, 2006).

The Ingram Coutts experience with *Quack This Way* seems to support this. Yet the lesson was possibly different for a few other titles, such as *Original People, Original Television*, which saw sales comparable to what books from academic publishers achieve. Why couldn't academic vendors find more books like that?

It's not as if academic librarians are completely satisfied with the books they buy from mainstream publishers. Evidence to the contrary isn't difficult to find, in fact, such as a reference to one publisher's "business model of charging outrageous prices for embarrassingly bad books," such as this librarian's example priced at "$145 for a collection of unrelated and apparently unedited essays," a book that nonetheless claimed 86 WorldCat holdings at libraries, "including mine" (Geffert, 2011). The librarian did not name the book in his essay; but, as with any new title from an established academic publisher, libraries would have expected their academic vendors to treat it not too differently from how they would treat a Pulitzer Prize winner.

Quack This Way and *Original People, Original Television* both received more vetting than that by Ingram Coutts, where there were no customer expectations of such treatment. Instead, staff sought out or noticed these two books and chose to offer them to customers solely on merit. How many more books like this pair are available today? Probably quite a few, although the effort in finding and evaluating them would, once more, not be small. One thing Ingram Coutts didn't do was to market to customers that certain titles were receiving this level of evaluation. Application of the term "self-published," from the company's bibliographic lexicon, was certainly a negative for the books. Hand-selected by staff, the term should have been a seal of quality, not a warning label. Instead, since most library profiles are very restrictive in this category, in line with traditional librarian attitudes, the staff's vetting efforts were undermined by normal operating procedures.

The trick for vendors will be to prevent normal operating procedures, and traditional attitudes, from getting in the way of good self-published books coming to the attention of their customers. Library vendors having a direct relationship with a self-publishing platform, such as Ingram Coutts has with IngramSpark, should explore how this might be turned to advantage in attracting authors to the platform, in developing more useful metadata, in identifying pertinent books for libraries, academic and public both, and in persuading interested libraries that a different pricing model might be in order than that for normal services. Attempting to survey the entire self-publishing universe seems a daunting project, but intracompany efforts are a possible way to build the model Whole Foods has perfected for grocery stores.

That same cross-company collaboration might also serve vendors well in addressing a new trend in libraries and self-publishing, that is, "to consider the public's interest in self-publishing as a service opportunity rather than a collection development concern" (Hadro, 2013). Public libraries are starting programs across the country aimed at helping local authors to write and publish their books (Staley, 2015). Some academic libraries, Indiana University being an example, have also begun programs to support campus authors looking for help in publishing a book (Dunham & Walters, 2014–2015). While these authors are normally young scholars needing to publish their first book with an academic press, many other campus authors have no need to strive for tenure and promotion and simply want to make their book available. In the years ahead, growing interest in the digital humanities, continued spread in awareness of open access, and the rise of library-based publishing, not to mention continued economic pressures on traditional scholarly book publishing, are likely to lead to more nontraditional academic publishing, some of it in the traditional form of the book. Vendors able to go beyond simply selling self-published books, but also offering services to help publish them, would seem to have a niche in this new local publishing ecology.

In today's self-publishing explosion, the winners so far have been the many thousands of now-published authors who can truly call themselves that; the companies who built the platforms enabling their authorship; and the online sites, led as always by Amazon, that generated sales for some of those authors. Everyone else whose livelihood has to do with books is still trying to figure things out. Even editors at the *New York Times Book Review* are not unaffected. Rachel Donadio of the *NYTBR* wrote an amusing essay on the "collective graphomania" leading so many Americans to sound "their barbaric yawps over the roofs of the world, as good old Walt Whitman, himself a self-published author, once put it." Donadio described a few of the "dozens" of odd self-published books submitted weekly by hopeful writers. "There's a lot of noise out there, and some of it is music," she wrote in conclusion, sounding hopeful herself (Donadio, 2008). Library book vendors, in this same new, noisy world, are also among the hopeful.

NOTES

1. According to searches of the Library of Congress catalog, OCLC WorldCat, and Amazon, performed January 1, 2015. The AMICUS catalogue of Library and Archives Canada does not offer a publisher search.

2. As of January 1, 2015.

3. Profiles are structured descriptions of library interests maintained by vendors to operate approval plans, new title notification services, and patron-driven acquisition programs.

4. This data was discussed by the author at the 2014 Charleston Conference in a presentation entitled *Self-Published Content and Approval Plans.*

5. All of these searches were performed on January 2, 2015.

6. The "ProQuest Dissertations and Theses Full Text" database already has nine entries with "David Foster Wallace" as an identifier/keyword, according to a search on January 3, 2015.

7. Whether or not Garner attempted that is unknown.

REFERENCES

About Bryan A. Garner. *LawProse.* (2012). Retrieved from https://www.lawprose .org/bryan_garner/about.php

Alter, A. (2011, December 9). How I became a best-selling author. *Wall Street Journal.* Retrieved from http://www.wsj.com/articles/SB100014240529702 04770404577082303350815824

Book and Periodical Council. (2015). The resource file. Grants. Retrieved from http://www.thebpc.ca/the-resource-file/grants/

Bosquet, M. (2013, May 6). A self-publication gold rush? *The Chronicle of Higher Education.* Retrieved from http://chronicle.com/article /A-Self-Publication-Gold-Rush-/139033/

Bowker. (2014). Self-publishing in the United States, 2008–2013: Print and ebook. Retrieved from http://bit.ly/selfpub13

Bradley, J., Fulton, B., & Helm, M. (2012). Self-published books: An empirical snapshot. *The Library Quarterly, 82*(2), 107–140.

Cuyahoga County Public Library is first library in Ohio to launch SELF-e digital self-publishing platform. (2014, October 22). *PRWeb.* Retrieved from http:// www.prweb.com/releases/2014/10/prweb12269639.htm

David, J. (2012). *Original people, original television.* Ottawa, ON: Debwe Communications.

David, J. (2015). Jennifer David, writer. Retrieved from http://debwe.ca/?page_id=2

Dilevko, J., & Dali, K. (2006). The self-publishing phenomenon and libraries. *Library & Information Science Research, 28,* 208–234.

Donadio, R. (2008, April 27). You're an author? Me too! *New York Times Book Review,* p. 27.

Dunham, G., & Walters, C. (2014, December–2015, January). From university press to the university's press: Building a one-stop campus resource for scholarly publishing. *Against the Grain, 26*(6), 28–30.

Enis, M. (2014, May 22). Smashwords and OverDrive ink distribution agreement. *Library Journal.* Retrieved from http://www.thedigitalshift.com/2014/05/ebooks/smashwords-overdrive-ink-distribution-agreement/

Garner, B. (2013). *Quack this way: David Foster Wallace and Bryan A. Garner talk language and writing.* Dallas, TX: RosePen Books.

Geffert, B. (2011, March 20). Libraries, publishers, and a plea for shotgun weddings. *The Chronicle of Higher Education.* Retrieved from http://chronicle.com/article/Libraries-Publishinga/126755/

Gregoire, C. (2014, April 16). David Foster Wallace on the key to living a compassionate life. *Huffington Post.* Retrieved from http://www.huffingtonpost.com/2014/04/16/david-foster-wallace-keny_n_5148773.html

Hadro, J. (2013, April 11). What's the problem with self-publishing? *Library Journal.* Retrieved from http://lj.libraryjournal.com/2013/04/publishing/whats-the-problem-with-self-publishing/#_

Herther, N. (2013, September–October). Today's self-publishing gold rush complicates distribution channels. *Online Searcher, 37(5),* 22–26.

Kenney, B. (2013). What we buy now: A look at purchasing trends in public libraries. *Publishers Weekly, 260*(3), 18–19.

Max., D. T. (2012). *Every love story is a ghost story: A life of David Foster Wallace.* New York, NY: Viking.

Max, D. T. (2013, December 11). D. F. W.'s favorite grammarian. *The New Yorker.* Retrieved from http://www.newyorker.com/books/page-turner/d-f-w-s-favorite-grammarian

Nixon, J., Freeman, R., & Ward, S. (Eds.). (2014). *Patron-driven acquisitions: Current successes and future directions.* London: Routledge.

Petrick, J. (2013). *Hidden in plain sight: The other people in Norman Rockwell's America.* Miami, FL: Informed Decisions Publishing.

Petrick, J. (2015). Books by Jane Allen Petrick. Retrieved from http://www
.janeallenpetrick.com/books-by-jane-allen-petrick/Hidden-in-Plain-Sight
-The-Other-People-in-Norman-Rockwells-America.html

Sargent, B. (2014, July 28). Surprising self-publishing stats. *Publishers Weekly*.
Retrieved from http://www.publishersweekly.com/pw/by-topic/authors/pw
-select/article/63455-surprising-self-publishing-statistics.html

Schiesel, J. (1973). *The Otis Redding story*. Garden City, NY: Doubleday.

Schwartz, M. (2013, July 11). Baker & Taylor owner buys Bookmasters; companies form strategic partnership. *Library Journal*. Retrieved from http://
lj.libraryjournal.com/2013/07/publishing/baker-companies-form-strategic
-partnership/#_

Scott, D. (2013, June). Can libraries survive the e-book revolution? *Govern-
ing*. Retrieved from http://www.governing.com/mag/july-2013-table-of
-contents.html

SelfPub 2.0. (2013). Purdue University, Purdue e-Pubs. Charleston Library Conference.
Retrieved from http://docs.lib.purdue.edu/charleston/2013/Communication/8/

Staley, L. (2015, January–February). Leading self-publishing efforts in communities. *American Libraries, 46*(1/2), 18–19.

Stewart, J. (2014, May 23). Norman Rockwell's art, once sniffed at, is becoming prized. *New York Times*. Retrieved from http://www.nytimes
.com/2014/05/24/business/norman-rockwell-captures-the-art-markets-eye
.html?emc=eta1&_r=0

Swords, David A. (Ed.). (2011). *Patron-driven acquisitions: History and best practices*. Berlin: De Gruyter Saur.

Toronto Public Library. (2015). Information for self-published authors. Retrieved
from http://www.torontopubliclibrary.ca/about-the-library/business-with
-the-library/self-published-authors.jsp

Whole Foods Market. (2014). Quality standards. Retrieved from http://www
.wholefoodsmarket.com/about-our-products/quality-standards

7 | Ingram and Independent Publishing

Robin Cutler, Ingram Content Group

INTRODUCTORY NOTE

There are many companies that offer services for independent publishers, but Ingram is unique in the marketplace in that it combines the broadest global distribution of both print and e-book content coupled with print-on-demand (POD) services. Retailers like Amazon, Barnes & Noble, Apple, and Kobo, to name a few, offer services and programs aimed at independent publishers to aid in the creation and distribution of authors' content through their specific Web sites. There are also many author services companies such as Author Solutions and Lulu that also assist authors in developing and distributing content. But since most of these companies use Ingram's distribution platform as part of their own service, this chapter focuses exclusively on Ingram.

EVOLUTION OF INGRAM CONTENT GROUP

Throughout its 50-year history, Ingram has been the dominant provider of book distribution services to all market segments from all content providers including independent publishers. In the early days, this market segment was often disparaged in the industry with such descriptors as "small, vanity, one-book wonders, micro, self-publishers." The authors usually fell into this category after suffering through multiple rejections at the hands of established agents and publishers who served as gatekeepers for content that could make it onto bookshelves and ultimately into the hands of readers. Having no alternative, these independent publishers forged ahead with the dream of seeing their books in the hands of readers and on the shelves of their local booksellers and libraries. This, of course, was the dark ages some 15 years ago before the Internet turned traditional publishing on its ear. But even in those early days, Ingram was a friend to independent publishers in helping them bring their books to market. Today, Ingram Content Group's commitment to independent publishers remains stronger than ever.

From its humble beginnings as a textbook depository, Ingram is now universally regarded as the leader in helping content reach its destination anywhere in the world. Whether the content is digital or physical, Ingram delivers to mobile phones, tablets, online retailers, bookstores, libraries, schools, and consumers across the globe. The company is on the cutting edge of technology in automated manufacturing, digital content distribution, and e-learning platforms and is trusted by publishers, retailers, and libraries for digital and physical solutions.

For independent publishers to have access to the world's largest and most trusted book distributor is no small thing. Ingram always made it possible for publishers of all sizes to provide metadata of their books that would be included in Ingram's database and ordering platform, called ipage®, which was made available to retailers and libraries. Publishers would then provide inventory of those books that would be shipped into the various Ingram warehouses. When retailers ordered a publisher's title, the order would be fulfilled out of that inventory; and then the publisher would be compensated on the sale after a wholesale discount was applied. Ingram would reorder from publishers based on retail and library orders through ipage. This was the standard operating procedure for decades, but the process left gaps between supply and demand that was particularly maddening for independent publishers who had little experience in forecasting demand and in managing the supply chain. Often these publishers would get an Ingram order stemming from a large bookstore chain but wouldn't have enough inventory on hand or have the cash needed to rush a reprint. Lost sales and missed opportunities plagued the industry for vendor, retailer, library, and content provider alike. This was the state of publishing for decades, even centuries. The most successful publishers were the ones who made the best educated guesses concerning their inventory and the demand for it.

PRINT ON DEMAND AND INDEPENDENT PUBLISHERS

Seeing this as a real problem that needed a solution, Ingram in 1996 made the herculean decision to invest in and implement technologies to make it possible to print and distribute small book orders from digital content files to help close the gap between supply and demand. In that year, Ingram launched Lightning Source (LSI), a print-on-demand (POD) company intended to help traditional publishers remove the guesswork on their slower selling inventory and to keep backlist titles perpetually in stock. But for independent publishers, the launch of Lightning Source was truly revolutionary and marked a profound change in the industry that would never again return to the traditional way of doing things.

"Lightning Source has exceeded my great expectations, charting new directions for the book industry," said John R. Ingram, chair of Ingram Content Group and founder of Lightning Source. "The unbeatable combination of quality print with our distribution engine has fueled enormous growth and success for the entire book supply chain—authors, publishers, wholesalers, distributors, retailers, and book buyers."

Recognized with numerous innovation awards in the company's 19-year history, Lightning Source–Ingram today produces more than one million books per month in multiple locations throughout the world including four in the United States and one each in the United Kingdom, France, and Australia. Additionally, the print footprint has expanded through its Global Connect network of printers in Germany, Russia, Brazil, and Poland with many more countries planned for the future. These print facilities put the manufacturing and shipping process of the book closer to the end consumer, reducing time and costs. This state-of-the-art technology allows publishers to produce content in a range of trim sizes, color options, and both paperback and hard covers. Additional flexibility extends to order management where content owners can order from one copy to 10,000 copies that can be shipped directly to the end customer. For retail and library orders through Ingram, the books are manufactured as orders are received; and then the publisher is compensated after the wholesale discount and print fees have been subtracted. This process removes the risk of a publisher having to pay for manufacture prior to an order being received.

Coupled with the largest book distribution network of more than 39,000 wholesale, retail, and library partners, Ingram has made it possible for independent publishers to greatly enhance their reach while reducing the financial commitment of bringing a book to market. Basically, Ingram has created a "pay as you go" model for independent publishers by providing them the ability to test the demand for their content at a fraction of the cost of the traditional model. What this has done in reality has been to turn single-book authors into business owner/publishers of their content. Many evolve into full-fledged publishing companies that then help other writers create and distribute their work.

DIGITAL ASSET MANAGEMENT AND DISTRIBUTION SERVICES

Print technology, coupled with distribution, is just one of the innovations Ingram has launched in the past few decades. Ingram was an early innovator in creating a digital content management service called CoreSource. But since distribution is what Ingram does best, it wasn't long before asset management was coupled with the broadest network of online retailers in the industry. Today, thousands of publishers and distributors worldwide—from multinationals to independents—use CoreSource to automate distribution of digital content to as many business partners as possible. In 2014 CoreSource made more than 65 million successful distributions of content, making it the market leader. The distribution network of more than 70 online retailers including Amazon Kindle, Apple iBooks, Barnes & Noble Nook, and Kobo is the largest global network in the world for e-book content.

PUBLISHING INDUSTRY CONTRACTION AND EXPANSION

The reality of the publishing industry was that for decades fewer books and authors were being published in the traditional way. With book agents and traditional trade publishers earning 90% of their revenue on 10% of authors with blockbuster hits, it became more and more risky and increasingly difficult for them to put resources into bringing unproven authors to market. In tandem, retailer Amazon continued to gain market share for readers who were more frequently browsing and purchasing their content online rather than through their neighborhood bookseller. As a result, for nearly a decade, there were more announcements of store closings than openings. Authors wanting to publish traditionally were finding it increasingly difficult with fewer options on both the publishing and retail side of things. Their last resort was to self-publish their work. And they did so in record numbers.

The publishing of e-book content started to explode in 2008 in conjunction with the evolution of e-readers in the marketplace (Kindle, Nook, and Kobo, to name a few). Publishing pundits proclaimed the end of printed books while e-book growth charted in the double digits for the next few years. Independent publishers, in particular, started flooding e-book platforms with content distributed to customers via their new e-readers. With the launch of the phenomenally successful Apple products (iPhone in 2007, iPad in 2010), readers had even more choices in consuming their e-content. It looked like a steady ramp upward with no end in sight.

SELF-PUBLISHING BEGINS TO MATURE

But starting in 2012, e-book sales started to decelerate from the double-digit growth pattern the industry experienced since 2008. Flattening of the e-book sales line continued into 2014. On the other hand, print sales volume grew like never before and was certainly far from dead as a preferred format for readers. This was especially good news for independent booksellers who had not only weathered the e-book bonanza but now appeared to be growing in numbers. More new bookstore openings were being announced than store closings.

Bowker, the official ISBN agency in the United States and publisher of *Books in Print*, announced in its "2014 Report on Self-Publishing in the U.S.": "A new analysis of U.S. ISBN data reveals that the number of self-published titles in 2013 increased to more than 458,564, up 17 percent over 2012 and 437 percent over 2008. Print titles were up a very strong 29 percent over 2012, indicating the format's continuing relevance to self-publishers. Print books have strong value to self-published authors, enabling them to reach a broad audience, often via independent bookstores."

Bowker also said, "While self-publishing continues to grow, the pace appears to be normalizing after several explosive years." Beat Barblan, Bowker director of identifier services, offered this analysis: "Our general conclusion is that self-publishing is beginning to mature. While it continues to be a force to reckon with, it is evolving from a frantic, wild west–style space to a more serious business. The market is stabilizing as the trend of self-publisher as business-owner, rather than writer only, continues."

INGRAM EMBRACES INDIE PUBLISHING

Even before the launch of Lightning Source (LSI) in 1996, Ingram had worked with small publishers who had 10 titles or more. But as LSI continued to develop POD technology and to gain wide adoption by mainstream publishing houses as a way to keep their backlist content in stock, more and more single-title authors and micro publishers discovered the benefits of POD. The quality POD product that LSI produced became harder and harder to distinguish from traditionally printed books. Word of mouth about Lightning Source spread at author workshops and conferences as a way to manufacture and bring a book to market with minimal financial investment.

As more self-publishers came to LSI, the company grappled with how to best support one-book authors who had no real knowledge of the publishing industry. Many had no computer skills and didn't have a real understanding of publishing processes like editing, design, and formatting content for digital printing. On top of this, providing all of the financial information needed to establish an LSI account could be a chore. Despite the complexity, from 1996 to 2012, tens of thousands of self-publishers completed the account sign-up process and uploaded their content for print manufacture and channel distribution. But this customer segment constantly had to adapt to a system that was created for a traditional publisher and backlist content.

INGRAMSPARK IS LAUNCHED

No one had to tell Ingram that self-publishing was becoming the fastest-growing segment in the publishing industry since they had been watching that segment grow since the launch of LSI. They also knew that continuing to direct these customers through a traditional publishing model was going to be frustrating for many. In part as an initiative John Ingram launched in 2013 called "Making It Easier to Do Business with Ingram," the company made the decision to develop a new portal specifically designed with indie publishers in mind. The new portal was christened "IngramSpark" and was unveiled at BookExpo America in June 2013.

> IngramSpark is the only publishing platform that delivers fully integrated print and digital distribution services to the book industry through a single source. What does that mean? Once you finish and format your book we make it possible to share it with the world. (From the IngramSpark portal)

THE IMPORTANCE OF DISTRIBUTION

IngramSpark allows indie publishers to quickly set up a free account, a process that was greatly streamlined down to just a few minutes from the weeks it could take to set up an account with LSI. Essentially, the new portal married the POD functionality and distribution from Lightning Source with the functionality and distribution of Ingram's e-book platform, CoreSource. Together with Ingram's distribution, IngramSpark provides indie publishers with a powerful and comprehensive way to manage digitally their print content and most importantly have access to the largest book distribution network in the world.

The reason distribution is so important for indie publishers is that most booksellers and certainly libraries typically will not order directly from these content providers because of all the complexities involved. It is far more convenient and beneficial for retailers to order from a wholesaler like Ingram that can supply content from thousands of different publishers. To get a book into most bookstores requires that a publisher provide a discount off the list price of the book and also that the book be returnable. Returnability is also a key factor for a bookstore in making a purchasing decision. This removes their risk if the book doesn't sell. Setting a book up as nonreturnable almost guarantees that bookstores won't carry it. It's not a stretch to imagine the complexity for a bookstore managing thousands of books from as many different publishers to understand the value added by a wholesaler/distributor such as Ingram. This is exactly the role that Ingram plays in the industry—being the center hub of the very complex publishing wheel.

PRICING, DISCOUNTING, RETURNABILITY, AND ORDERING BOOKS

Obviously, for indie publishers to have their books listed with Ingram is one of the key strategies in setting a title up for success in the marketplace. And not just in the U.S. market, but in other global markets that Ingram serves. IngramSpark publishers determine the suggested retail list price for their titles in all markets. If pricing is not submitted, the title will be unavailable for sale in that market.

Many first-time indie publishers find the pricing of their books to be one of the most daunting challenges. To help with this, it's recommended that publishers do their homework by visiting local booksellers or online retail sites for comparable books in size, format, and subject matter to gauge how best to price their own books. Remember that prices can always be changed even after publication.

In order to make titles available to both physical and online retailers, publishers offer a discount off the retail price of their titles. This discount represents the profit in selling the book for both the store and Ingram. The wholesale trade discount most publishers choose to offer booksellers is 55%. However, IngramSpark does provide the option of setting a discount within the range of 30–35% (minimum) to 55% (maximum). Applying a discount of less than 55% can possibly limit the sale of a title to booksellers; this, however, may be the right choice for many publishers depending on their sales strategies.

Publishers also determine the returnability of their titles. IngramSpark currently offers publishers three title-level returns options, as follows:

- Non-returnable: IngramSpark will not accept returns from booksellers for any title so designated.
- Return/Deliver: Allows titles to be sold on a returnable basis. Returned books will be sent back to the content provider for a fee.
- Return/Destroy: Allows titles to be sold on a returnable basis but no shipping and handling fees will apply. IngramSpark will destroy any returned books that it receives if this option is selected.

Content listed in IngramSpark is made available for ordering to Ingram's 39,000 retail and library partners. These orders are called "wholesale orders." In the case of wholesale orders, the publisher is paid the list price minus the discount they set on the book. In the case of a print order, the cost of printing is also deducted from compensation paid to the publisher for the order. As an example:

Order Type: Wholesale—order 1 copy
Book Type: 250 page, 6 x 9, paperback book
List Price: $22.00
Retail Discount: 55%
Net Price: 1 – (List Price x discount) = $9.90
Print fee[1] = $3.80
Publisher Compensation on this order would be $6.10

IngramSpark also encourages publishers to place orders for their own books that can be manufactured and shipped back to their own warehouse or dropshipped directly to their customer. This is known as a "publisher direct or dropship order." In the case of these orders, the publisher pays only print and shipping fees (no discount is applied). The beauty of this service is that indie publishers don't have to maintain a warehouse or have books stacked in their garage. They don't have to invest in packing supplies or have to manage the packing of boxes of heavy books.

INGRAMSPARK CONTENT SUBMISSION GUIDELINES

Of course, before content can be sold, it must first be uploaded into the IngramSpark portal so that it can be processed, printed, and then distributed. There are a few rules that must be followed to ensure the successful processing of content:

- IngramSpark ingestion is fully automated. There is little or no human intervention as the files process through our system.
- Files must be formatted and submitted according to the *IngramSpark File Creation Guide* that can be found at https://www1.ingramspark.com /Portal/Help
- All versions of a title that will be distributed must be supplied with a unique ISBN13 number. For example, the print *paperback* must be submitted under its own unique ISBN13 that is different from the print *hardback* edition. Likewise, the eBook edition would have its own unique ISBN13 that is different from the print editions.
- When an updated or revised file is uploaded for a title already submitted to IngramSpark, the new version replaces the older version. The new file goes through the same ingestion process as the original and will be the version distributed to our retail partners for purchase or download.

For indie publishers, formatting content can be one of the most frustrating parts in the publishing process. If publishers are not experienced in creating digital content or don't have access to book layout software, IngramSpark recommends enlisting the help of a professional book designer. It's also recommended that a professional copyeditor review the manuscript before the design phase begins.

File Requirements for Print Distribution

For every print title, two files should be uploaded consisting of one complete interior file[2] (formatted as .pdf) and one complete cover file[3] (formatted as .pdf).

PDF File Checklist (for POD titles)

The following list contains basic guidelines to help avoid what we've found to be the most common causes of file rejection and delays for content formatted for POD.

Interior Files

- Must be uploaded as a separate file from the cover. *Please note that PDFs created using the "save as" function from MS Word are not supported.*
- Use single-page format (1-up per page).
- Do not include crop, registration, or printer marks.
- All fonts must be embedded.
- Make sure the final page is blank.
- Margins must be a minimum of 0.5" (13 mm) from final trim size on all sides. This includes page numbers and non-bleeding text and art. We allow for a 1/16" (0.0625 in / 2 mm) variance in printing. If text/images are too close to the trim edges, they could be cut in the printing and binding process.
- Gutter Margin (no ink area): 0.125" (3 mm) is required on the bind side of interior. Saddle stitch books (anything less than 48 pgs.) do not require gutter margins.
- Bleed: B&W interior—We do not guarantee bleed off of any edge of the text page. Color interior—Full 0.125" (3 mm) past final trim size, except on bind/spine side.
- Spot Colors: B&W interior—Do not include spot colors or ICC profiles and all images should be converted to grayscale.
- Color interior—Must include CMYK images at 72 dpi or higher. CMYK value should not exceed 240%. Elements should not be built in "Registration." All spot colors with/without transparencies must be converted to CMYK.
- For revisions, the entire file must be re-uploaded. Partial pages cannot be accepted.

Cover Files

- To ensure accuracy, use the IngramSpark custom template generator tool—located under the "Tools" section of the web site. Simply fill in the required fields and a custom template will be emailed to you.
- Must be uploaded as a separate PDF from the interior. PDFs created using the "save as" function from MS Word are not supported. Barcodes are mandatory on all covers. 100% black only and placed on a white box/background.
- Resolution: 300 dpi (dots per inch) LPI (lines per inch): 180 Color Space: CMYK.
- Bleed: 0.125" (3 mm) on all four sides.
- Type safety: 0.25" (6 mm) minimum on all sides.
- Spine Type Safety: For page counts below 48, spine text is not available. Spines 0.35" and larger—0.0625" (2 mm) left/right sides. Spines smaller than 0.35"—0.03125" (1 mm) left/right sides.
- Text that is 24 pt. or below, please use 100% black only.
- All spot colors with/without transparencies must be converted to CMYK.

File Requirements for E-Book Distribution to Online E-Retailers

For every e-book title, two files should be uploaded consisting of one complete Interior EPUB (formatted as .epub) and one complete front cover (formatted as .jpeg or .jpg).

E-Book File Checklist

Interior Files

- Size: 100 MB or less. (Please note, while IngramSpark and retail sites can accept 100 MB files, the IDPF Validator cannot check files over 10 MB due to the amount of time it would take.)
- Format: EPUB 2 or 3 (flowable text only). Sorry, we cannot accept fixed format or enhanced EPUB files at this time.
- No single image inside an EPUB can be greater than 3.2 million pixels. (Total pixels = length in pixels x width in pixels.)
- Include an internal cover image. This should be formatted the same size of, and as part of your interior. (For use within the book content.)

- Be sure the metadata entered in IngramSpark matches the information on the cover. For example, if the cover title is *Paradiso*, but the metadata is for *Purgatorio*, then the items do not match.
- There should not be any reference to page numbers in the book. This includes the Table of Contents. Your e-book will never look just like your print book. E-readers are limited in the way they display content and your book will appear different from device to device.

Cover Files for Display Use on Retail Partners' Web Sites

- File must contain front cover only. Full spread print book jackets that include spine and back cover will be rejected.
- Format: Must be a JPG File.
- Size: 2560 pixels on longest side. Minimum 1600 pixels on shortest side.
- Color: All front covers must be RGB.
- The content of the cover image must not infringe another publisher's or artist's copyright on the same cover.

LIBRARIES AND BOOKSTORES AS INDIE PUBLISHERS

One of the trends we're starting to see at Ingram is that libraries and bookstores are taking an active role in assisting self-publishers in addition to publishing original content of their own. With the tools now available through a service like IngramSpark, launching a publishing program has never been easier. Since libraries and bookstores have always been a community's best resource in the publishing industry, it was just a matter of time before they took on the roles of advisor and publisher.

Two examples of this trend are worth mentioning here: Williamson County Public Library in Tennessee and Village Books in Bellingham, Washington. Williamson County Public Library, under the direction of Dolores Greenwald, decided to publish a picture book featuring popular local miniature horses, Bucky and Bonnie, to help introduce children to the library. "The motivation . . . was the desire for the library to move in the direction of being content creators, not just content curators," said Greenwald. Written and designed by library staff and published under the library's imprint,

Academy Park Press, the title was printed and distributed by IngramSpark. *Bucky and Bonnie's Library Adventure* became a local hit garnering both publicity and fundraising opportunities, especially when the real-life horses made appearances in the library to sign books. The library has since published *Bullets and Bayonets: A Battle of Franklin Primer*, which has won awards and been adopted by the local school board. They also have launched an awards program for local authors where winners receive library training and support in publishing their own works via IngramSpark.

Village Books, seeing the industry growth in independent publishing, has incorporated services directly in the store to help authors self-publish their work. As Village Book's publishing director, Brendan Clark, has noted, "Our publishing program brings together flexible project management, high-quality on-demand book production, and the expertise of local professionals, all with the unified goal of helping authors get their books in print." To date, Village Books has published dozens of books, some of which are best sellers for IngramSpark.

INDEPENDENT PUBLISHER CONTENT AND LIBRARIES

Of course, one of the challenges today is that only a fraction of independently published content is making its way onto the shelves or databases of libraries. This is true even for academic content written by scholars in their field. Traditionally, libraries rely on review media such as *Library Journal, Publishers Weekly, Kirkus,* and *Choice* to help guide their acquisition choices. Since only a handful of titles end up being reviewed, there's a huge mass of content not being adequately vetted. At Ingram, a process is being created and tested that would properly vet nonfiction content published through IngramSpark via staff specialists in Ingram's Library Services/ Coutts program. Content deemed appropriate or that matches the collection development profile would be brought to the attention of the library. To help with the vetting process, additional metadata is being collected as a title is being set up in IngramSpark that would identify an author's professional background and affiliations, prior publications and reviews, geographic location, and the unique aspect of the work in terms of other books in the field. This initiative is just getting under way in 2015.

APPENDIX: INGRAMSPARK GLOSSARY OF PUBLISHING TERMS

Agency Price: The price at which Apple sells the title through iTunes. All prices must be in dollar increments that end in .99, except if you set the price for $0 (i.e., free).

Bar Code: A machine-readable image on the back of books to indicate ISBN and possibly the price. Bar codes are required by many retailers for print products that they carry. This can be in the form of an EAN (European Article Number) bar code, used for books, or a UPC (Universal Product Code) bar code, used more commonly in the U.S. for non-book products.

Content: The chapters or other formal divisions of a book or e-book.

Contributors: Up to three contributors (e.g., authors, editors, illustrators, etc.) may be identified with a book. These are saved and communicated to retailers via IngramSpark catalog information.

Copyright: A form of intellectual property, giving the creator of an original work exclusive rights to that work's publication, distribution, and adaptation for a certain time period. After the time period, the work is said to enter the public domain. For information on U.S. copyright laws, visit www.copyright.gov.

Description: This brief description of the book will be communicated to distribution partners who wish to describe and market the book on their Web site(s) and to their customers. We recommend that you provide a book description for all new books to assist booksellers in presenting your books to their customers. The book description should be at least 40 characters but should not exceed 4,000 characters including spaces. In addition, no HTML tagging, bullets, or other special formatting should be embedded.

Digital Rights Management (DRM): A system or technology used to place limitations (in regards to access or copying) onto digital content (books, movies, music, etc.). A publisher or author, not the retailer, determines the level of restrictions applied to it. This includes how many times content can be downloaded for a single purchase and the number of devices (computers, readers, etc.) to which the content can be transferred. DRM is usually administered by those that convert or sell the content.

Direct Store Programs: A web portal from e-retailers, such as Apple and Barnes & Noble, where you can upload your content and then post for sale only in their online store.

Distributor: A party that handles all fulfillment, credit, and collections on behalf of a publisher. A distributor looks for an exclusive agreement with the publisher within geographic areas and types of markets and, therefore, is likely to stock all titles from a publisher in their warehouse. In the case of the book industry, a distributor would sell to retailers and to wholesalers.

Download: The act of transferring a file from the Internet to your computer or mobile device.

E-Retailer (Online Retailer): An online retailer that sells books, both physical and digital, and often other related merchandise to readers. E-retailers source their products from various players in the supply chain including publishers, wholesalers, distributors, and fulfillment companies.

Edition: Version of a work. A new edition means that there have been a series of corrections and/or a new feature added (such as a preface, appendix, or additional content), or that the content has been revised.

Electronic Book/E-Book: Digital equivalent of a conventional printed book. E-books are read on personal computers, smartphones, or readers. There are many formats available; some can be used on multiple devices while others are only available on certain devices.

EPUB (.epub): Proposed format from the International Digital Publishing Forum. ".epub" is the file extension of an XML format for digital books and publications. EPUB reflows content, so that text can be optimized for the display screen being used at the time.

File Transfer Protocol (FTP): A way to transfer files to and from Web sites without using a browser. Usually requires FTP client software.

Fulfillment: The process of filling orders. Fulfillment firms usually provide storage, pick, pack, and ship services for publishers. A company can also offer file creation, storage, and delivery to online retailers or e-books. Could also be called Digital Distributor.

Imprint: An imprint is a trade name used by a publisher to identify a line of books or a publishing branch within the publishing organization. An imprint is distinguished from a corporate name in that it does not represent an entity with a corporate life of its own. The imprint appears on all books produced in the line. Imprints are optional and not required.

ISBN (International Standard Book Number): A unique 13-digit number provided by your country's ISBN agency and assigned by the publisher to identify a particular format, edition, and publisher of a book. ISBNs are used worldwide as a unique identifier for each book title/format combination. They are used to simplify distribution and purchase of books throughout the global supply chain.

.JPG or .JPEG (Joint Photographic Experts Group): An image file format ideal for digital images with lots of colors, such as photographs and the cover image for your book.

Keywords: Single words or short phrases that describe your book and help improve search results.

Market (Channel): Bookselling outlets are often grouped by the type of customers they service. Examples include traditional bookstores (known as trade), big-box stores (e.g., Costco, Target, Wal-Mart), religious bookstores, gift stores, libraries, and educational accounts. E-commerce or sales through an online channel are another market channel.

Metadata: Details about your title that booksellers and buyers need to know. It includes details specific to a particular form of the book (e.g., price, hardcover, paperback, publication date) as well as general information that may apply to all forms of your work (e.g., author, description, table of contents).

Offset Printing: Printing on a traditional printing press where many copies of a book are produced at one time.

ONIX: The international standard for representing and communicating book industry product information via electronic form. This XML standard is commonly used by retailers, distributors, and wholesalers to communicate with each other about books that are available for sale.

On Sale Date: The date to determine when a book may be sold by retail partners.

Page Count: Page count is the total number of pages in the book, including blanks and front matter. The total number of pages must be evenly divisible by 2.

PDF (.pdf): A file format developed by Adobe to allow the creation and sharing of documents that will look and print the same on any machine.

Print on Demand (POD): Printing, usually from a digital file to a digital printer. In this case, the physical book is only printed when it is ordered. The exact number of copies ordered is what is printed. No extra copies are kept on warehouse shelves.

Publication Date: The date on which a retail consumer or library may take possession of a product.

Publisher: The entity that owns the legal right to make the product available. This can be the same entity as the author, a company formed by the author or a group of authors to publish their own works, a self-publishing service provider that assists the author in bringing the book to market, or a traditional publishing company that purchases the right to publish a work from an author.

Reprint: A new batch of printed copies without substantial changes.

Retailer: A store that sells books, and often other related merchandise, to readers. Retailers source their products from various players in the supply chain including publishers, wholesalers, and distributors.

Returns: Historically, publishers grant booksellers the right to return unwanted and/or overstocked copies of books. These books are considered "returnable." As books are returned, booksellers charge publishers for the cost (i.e., their purchase price) of any books returned and expect to be reimbursed. The cost of returned books is either deducted or netted against the proceeds of book sales of the publishers' titles in the month returns are shipped to the publisher. IngramSpark supports standard industry conventions by allowing publishers to designate whether or not their titles can be returned. The publisher can make this designation at the time of initial title setup.

IngramSpark allows you to change the return designations of a title at any time after initial title submission with 45 days prior written notice. You have the ability to change the return designation from your Dashboard. Select "Edit" and progress through to step number 4 of the process. Publishers may check the sales and returns activity of any or all titles at any time by logging into our publisher secure web site.

Status: Indicates the availability of the book. The book industry uses terms, such as forthcoming (going to be published in the future), active (available for purchase now), and publication cancelled (item will not be published now or in the future). When telling customers about your title, you may be asked to supply this information.

Subject: The IngramSpark distribution network partners use Subjects to categorize books. These categories briefly describe the content of a book. Retailers, distributors, and libraries require you to select at least one subject.

Suggested Retail Price: Publishers determine the suggested retail list price on all titles in all markets. If pricing is not submitted, the title will appear as unavailable for sale in that market.

Territory Right: The rights of a distributor, granted by the producer or supplier, to sell a product in a particular geographical area.

Title: The title information placed in this field will be used for all reporting and reseller catalog communications (where appropriate).

Trade: Refers to traditional bookselling channels including independent bookstores (e.g., a single store, a local group of stores) and chain bookstores (e.g., Barnes & Noble, Hastings, Books-a-Million).

Trade Discount: An amount or rate by which the catalog, list, or suggested retail price of an item is reduced when sold to a reseller. The trade discount reflects the reseller's profit margin.

Trading Terms (aka Publisher Discount): Each publisher will need to set trading terms with each customer. When selling to distributors, wholesalers, or retail bookstores, you are expected to quote a price that allows them to resell the book and make money on that sale. First, you will set the retail price (the price the reader buys at) for each geographic market in which the product is available. This can be expressed in the local currency or in USD. Then you will set the price at which the distributor, wholesaler, or retailer would purchase from you.

Wholesaler: A business that obtains books from publishers and their appointed distributors in order to fulfill orders for retailers and libraries. They offer non-exclusive distribution to publishers. Wholesalers will stock certain quantities of titles but will usually not warehouse your entire inventory. Wholesalers meet customer requests for packaging books across a set of publishers and deliver the goods quickly to meet retailer or library needs.

Sources: Ingram, Bowker, IBPA, and Lulu from the uPublishU Conference at
  BookExpo America, May 2013.

NOTES

1. To determine the actual print and shipping fees for any book that IngramSpark prints, go to: https://www1.ingramspark.com/Portal/Calculators/ShippingCalculator

2. Complete interior file: Included in the PDF would be every page that you see when you open a physical copy of a book. This includes any blank pages, whether they are numbered or not, from beginning to end. Individual PDFs of each chapter or parts do not make a "complete" book.

3. Complete cover PDF: This means all the information (text and images) on the front cover, back cover, spine, and flaps (if cover is a dust jacket) assembled into a single PDF. A PDF of the front cover alone is not a complete cover PDF.

8 | Review Sources of Interest to Librarians for Independently Published Books

Eleanor I. Cook, East Carolina University

INTRODUCTION

With the explosion of independently published (also known as self-published) books, it becomes very difficult for librarians interested in this material to identify the works that have the most appeal and are of the best quality. While public libraries are increasingly embracing self-published books these days, academic librarians still are reluctant to add them except very selectively, due to budgetary restraints, perceived lack of review mechanisms, and a continued impression that such works are inferior to traditionally published books. Self-published books primarily become known to readers through word-of-mouth, Internet sites such as Amazon.com, and social media avenues rather than through traditional review tools (which librarians really focus on). In fact, avid readers of indie books often completely bypass the library for discovery since these books are often readily available free or at a nominal price. Nonetheless, there is a role for libraries to play if they can somehow make order out of the chaos (Davis, 2014). Review options exist that focus on independently published books, and these should become familiar to librarians who want to include these kinds of materials in their collections. The review sources discussed in this chapter are included specifically for the consideration of librarians. The list is not meant to be exhaustive as there are new tools being developed constantly and others that may be too specialized for mention here.

AMAZON.COM REVIEWS (FROM READERS AND OTHER SOURCES)

Most independent authors (referred to in the popular press as "indie" authors) depend on Amazon reviews for building interest in their books because these reviews are readily available to the browsing public. The librarian's dilemma is that, while these reviews reflect the reading public's personal opinions of a book, they can be unreliably skewed or biased and, in some cases, completely misleading. An author's friends and family often weigh in with reviews that are posted to help the author regardless of the quality of the book. Conversely, harsh or unfair reviews may be contributed by individuals with some aversion to the material or with an ax to grind. Amazon designates certain reviewers as "Top Customer Reviewers." They review on a regular basis and are proven to be reliable and consistent in their reviewing habits (and there are thousands in this category). The usefulness of Amazon reader reviews derives from the convenience of having them right at hand if a prospective reader is about to decide whether to purchase the book. Controversial self-published books such as *My Parents Open Carry* (as an example) will attract dozens, if not hundreds, of comments and reviews that may be sarcastic or derisive, not to mention downright amusing on occasion.

Amazon also provides reviews from standard sources that librarians know and recognize. These are useful since having them shown at the Amazon site helps readers know that the independently published book has been recognized by the bibliographic press, which adds to the book's prestige. If a book is part of a specific genre, there will often be reviews available in publications devoted to that subject. Genre publications do a decent job of finding indie published books since they can identify them more easily, and authors who manage their own marketing usually know how to solicit reviews from these sources.

The other logistical dilemma for librarians is that looking for excellent self-published books on Amazon is like looking for needles in a haystack. The universe of independently published books on Amazon is vast. Amazon is best used for researching a specific title or list of titles that need vetting for a particular reason. For example, checking Amazon is a logical first step if a title has been brought to a librarian's attention by a local user or author and is not likely to be found in other review sources.

READER SOCIAL MEDIA SITES

Reader sites such as Goodreads are very popular and provide avid readers a place to discuss all kinds of books with kindred spirits. Goodreads has a group especially for librarians and also has specialized book groups and supporting features, including reviews. However, when Goodreads was purchased by Amazon in 2013, some authors and readers were dismayed. After this acquisition, changes were made in review policies that fueled controversy (Miller, 2013). There are a number of alternative sites, all of which may provide some utility to librarians seeking reviews of indie books, but again, may be more useful on a case-by-case basis ("Ten Top Alternative Sources," 2013).

INDIVIDUAL BLOGGERS

Self-published authors often do and probably should when possible reach out to individual bloggers who review indie books and have a following in the author's topic. There is a site called Indie View that registers and maintains (for free) a list of such bloggers. The list at this writing is not terribly long since identification is a word-of-mouth effort. Bloggers who review books are not necessarily easy for librarians to keep track of, but a collection development librarian who wants exhaustive coverage in a specific subject might want to keep tabs on this type of reviewer.

SITES THAT PROMOTE FREE AND INEXPENSIVE E-BOOKS (INCLUDING INDIE TITLES OF MERIT)

Web sites such as BookBub, BookGorilla, and The Fussy Librarian are e-book alert sites that tailor recommendations to a reader's designated interests and typically alert users to discounted pricing as well. These sites can be useful to librarians looking specifically for e-book formats but are not as relevant to those seeking print indie books. For an overview of these three sites, see the description on Standoutbooks.com, a support consultancy for indie authors (Hemus, 2013).

While it has become clear that independent authors consider traditional review publications to be less effective for their marketing goals than social media and other, more personal types of outreach to readers, the following are review sites that librarians may find useful.

FOREWORD REVIEWS AND FOREWORD CLARION REVIEWS

These review publications, available since 1998, emphasize reviews for "independent, alternative, university and self-publishing industries" (Web site). If an indie author's submission does not make the cut for *Foreword Reviews,* the author can opt to pay to be covered by *Clarion. Clarion Reviews* is a fee-based service ($305, 6–8 weeks). *Foreword* has a reputation for covering a large variety of small presses and independent publications, and they have a yearly awards program in which librarians and others in the book industry serve as jury judges (full disclosure: this author has served as a jury judge for these awards).

KIRKUS REVIEWS

Most librarians are familiar with *Kirkus* as it has been around for a very long time (founded in 1933). It is considered a core library reference resource. In recent times, *Kirkus* has begun to cater to self-published authors by offering fee-based reviews, which are selectively included in their publication and are designated as such. *Kirkus Reviews* is a subscription-based product; but, even if a library does not subscribe directly, the content is also indexed full-text in standard aggregator databases. *Kirkus Indie Reviews* are offered at two levels: Standard (7–9 weeks after submission) for $425.00 or Express (4–6 weeks after submission) for $575.00. For these fees, indie authors are told:

> If you choose to publish your review on our website, we will distribute it to our licensees, including Google, BN.com, Ingram, Baker & Taylor and more. On top of that, our editors will consider it for publication in *Kirkus Reviews* magazine, which is read by librarians, booksellers, publishers, agents, journalists and entertainment executives. Your review may also be selected to be featured in our email newsletter, which is distributed to more than 50,000 industry professionals and consumers. (Web site)

In addition, *Kirkus* provides authors with editorial and marketing services, also fee-based. There is a free general marketing guide available for download from the Web site. The monthly publication offers "Indie books of the month" and "Indie books of the year" rankings in different categories (fiction, nonfiction, etc.), which may be useful to librarians seeking purchasing guidance.

BLUEINK REVIEW

BlueInk Review has been around for a relatively short period (since 2010). This reviewing service is also fee-based, but its distinction is that it caters exclusively to self-published authors and aspires to be the "gold standard" reviewing source for this type of publication. The prices it charges authors are slightly less than *Kirkus* ($395 for the review to be completed in 7–9 weeks, or a fast track review, $495 for the review to be completed in 4–5 weeks) (Web site).

As of this writing, the reviews are freely accessible via the Web site, and librarians can sign up for an e-mail alert service for free. The reviews are reposted on other sites as well—for example, *Publishing Perspectives* features "starred" BlueInk reviews (Web site). The number of books that are featured monthly is manageable, and the reviews are well written. They offer a sort feature by region of the country that could be very useful if it actually worked—their search engine seems a bit clunky and needs refining. They track authors' home towns *and* current residences since these are not necessarily the same, although they do not seem to track fictional settings by region (this could also be useful to librarians seeking reviews of regional fiction). The question remains whether *BlueInk* will be able to maintain and/or increase their eyeball views since the other heavy hitters in the publishing world have entered the self-publishing review scene and may overwhelm this start-up.

PUBLISHERS WEEKLY'S BOOKLIFE.COM

While an indie author can submit a book to be reviewed by *PW* for free, these reviews are highly competitive and not guaranteed. The BookLife Web site also offers other types of paid author services. For example:

- First Read: $79—Submit your synopsis and 1st 1500 words of your manuscript; evaluation within 10 days of submission; one-shot; no follow-up; anonymous reviewer.
- Full service manuscript evaluation: Starting at $499; based on word count; evaluation within six weeks; one-shot; no follow-up; anonymous reviewer.
- PW Select: Promotion service: $149.

Every month, *Publishers Weekly* publishes *PW Select*, a supplement dedicated to covering the self-publishing industry that features interviews with authors, book announcements and listings, news, features, analysis, book reviews, and more. *PW Select* is also a marketing resource that provides tools to help you get your book noticed. (Web site)

LIBRARY JOURNAL'S COLLABORATION WITH BIBLIOBOARD: SELF-E

This collaboration is a unique effort that is still evolving. According to the SELF-e Web site:

SELF-e is an innovative collaboration between *Library Journal* and BiblioBoard that enables authors and libraries to work together to expose notable self-published ebooks to voracious readers looking to discover something new. If selected via *Library Journal's* SELF-e curation process, the author's ebooks will become part of a unique discovery platform for participating public libraries across the United States that enables patrons to read ebooks on any device, at any time. This free service is available to all self-published authors, no matter which self-publishing service(s) they use. (Web site)

Several states are working with this product to help promote their local authors. Examples can be found in California, Massachusetts (http://guides .masslibsystem.org/ebooks), Arizona (http://readingarizona.org/), and Ohio (http://www.cuyahogalibrary.org/Events/Writing-Programs/SELF-E.aspx) with others in development (Web site).

OTHER REVIEW SITES

Self-Publishing Review

SPR is yet another site offering self-published authors reviews for a fee. The prices are competitive and a bit lower than at the sites already covered above. They also provide additional author services similar to those already described.

IndieReader.com

Another site with similar services and competitive prices even lower than those described above.

Off the Bookshelf.com

Yet another support site for self-published authors—it doesn't really have a well-developed review mechanism, although it does list "recently added books" on its Web site.

NetGalley

NetGalley "provides digital review copies to professional readers, including booksellers, librarians, media, bloggers, reviewers and educators" (Web site). The books available for review are provided prepublication by a select number of publishers. However, NetGalley also makes indie titles available through a partnership with the Independent Book Publishers Association. Books are available for download to Kindles, Nooks, and a variety of other mobile devices and platforms. The window of opportunity for receiving a newly published book is relatively small, and not every book requested by a reviewer will be delivered. Reviewers are required to keep a profile page on the site so that publishers and authors can match books with reviewers. The site is a good place to get free copies of books you want to read, but there is no guarantee you'll get what you request; and the site really isn't geared for the purposes of collection development of self-published books.

WHAT CREDENCE TO GIVE PAID REVIEWS?

Self-published authors have uneven expectations and experiences with fee-based review sources. Independent authors may not have the money to pay for such services or balk at the very idea in principle. There are, however, testimonials from satisfied indie authors evident on many of the review Web sites though anecdotal evidence suggests at best, ambivalence, and at worst, a deep dissatisfaction with such models. And yet, these services, if proven effective, can add value to inexperienced authors' end products and give them needed visibility.

The offerings for independent publishing reviews are probably peaking, and the market will not be able to sustain all these entries. At some point, the options currently available will either fail or consolidate. As with any new market, there will be casualties.

HOW ARE LIBRARIANS TO DEAL WITH ALL THESE OPTIONS?

Library-related review sites have cautiously started reviewing self-published books. ALA's *Booklist*, for example, will now consider them, but they only review books that are prepublication (normally 16 weeks before publication). Self-published authors may not be aware of this policy and could miss the opportunity for consideration since they typically publish first and ask for reviews afterward. ACRL's *Choice*, which focuses exclusively on academic materials, states that they review such materials "very selectively" (Web site).

WHAT ABOUT LIBRARY BOOK VENDORS?

Major library book vendors are watching the scene carefully and are likely to participate once they develop business models that make it worth their while. This too is only a matter of time. Librarians are not demanding these services loudly yet, but they may in the near future. Public libraries in particular are already feeling pressure from local indie authors (hence the SELF-e project). Academic libraries have not shown as much interest.

Approval plans for traditionally published materials have been superseded in many cases by demand-driven acquisition (DDA) plans. Adding critically reviewed indie publications would enhance book vendor approval and DDA services if vendors can get a handle on the landscape well enough to add value. If librarians could depend on their book vendors to do the critical review vetting for them, they might be more willing to add indie published materials to their collections.

CONCLUSION

It's clear that independent publishing is changing the landscape of book creation, distribution, and reading; and, if libraries want to include these kinds of books in their collections, it will behoove them to demand appropriate review and selection services from their vendors in order to discover relevant and useful content. Finding methods for effectively separating the wheat from the chaff will be key. At this point, vendors have not found useful mechanisms to deal with the deluge; but they are aware that it is an area of growth they could take advantage of in the future.

REFERENCES

BlueInk Review Web site. Retrieved from http://www.blueinkreview.com/about

BookLife.com Web site. Retrieved from http://booklife.com/about-us/pw-select.html

Choice Web site. Retrieved from http://www.ala.org/acrl/choice/selectioncriteria

Davis, M. (2014, December 1). How libraries and patrons can beat publishers at publishing. Retrieved from https://www.linkedin.com/pulse/article/20141201194812 -11421233-how-libraries-and-patrons-can-beat-publishers-at-publishing

Foreword Reviews Web site. Retrieved from https://publishers.forewordreviews .com/reviews/

Hemus, A. (2013, December 23). BookBub vs. BookGorilla vs. The Fussy Librarian—Which is the best ebook marketing service? *Standoutbooks*. Retrieved from https://www.standoutbooks.com/bookbub-bookgorilla-fussy-librarian/

Kirkus Reviews Web site. Retrieved from https://www.kirkusreviews.com /author-services/indie/

Library Journal SELF-e Web site. Retrieved from http://reviews.libraryjournal .com/self-e/

Miller, L. (2013, October 23). How Amazon and Goodreads could lose their best readers. *Salon*. Retrieved from http://www.salon.com/2013/10/23 /how_amazon_and_goodreads_could_lose_their_best_readers/

NetGalley Web site. Retrieved from https://www.netgalley.com/

Publishing Perspectives Web site. Retrieved from http://publishingperspectives .com/tag/self-publishing/

SELF-e Library Partners. Current. Retrieved from http://self-e.libraryjournal .com/libraries/resources/

The ten top alternative sources for Goodreads. (2013, July–August). Supplemental content to: Goodreads: Social Media Meets Readers Advisory. *Online Searcher, 37*(4). Retrieved from http://www.infotoday.com/onlinesearcher /extras/Herther--GoodReads--Social-Media-Meets-Readers-Advisory.pdf

9 | Self-Publishing and Bibliographic Control

Robert P. Holley, Wayne State University

INTRODUCTION

This chapter will investigate the importance of bibliographic control for self-publishing, the current status of bibliographic control, and possible future steps. The number of self-published books has rapidly increased in the United States, accounting for at least 50% of all titles published, though accurate figure are difficult to determine in part because of the lack of bibliographic control in contrast with commercially published books (Bowker). Of course, though their numbers are greater, the sales volume of self-published materials is much less than that of commercial publications. Issues of their quality partially explain this disparity; but difficulties in discovery, distribution, inventory control, and library/bookstore processing limit the possibility for potentially popular self-published books to meet their market potential. More effective bibliographic control including both traditional cataloging and accurate metadata would help overcome these constraints and level the playing field with commercially published items.

THE IMPORTANCE OF BIBLIOGRAPHIC CONTROL

Bibliographic control has great importance for the success of publications for two principal reasons: discovery and distribution/handling. Librarians, publishers, and booksellers have come to depend upon sophisticated mechanisms that have developed over decades, if not centuries, to publicize, distribute, and find trade and university press publications. These mechanisms have become second nature so that many may not realize

113

how their minimal support for self-published books hampers their distribution to libraries and bookstores and thus lessens their availability to readers.

Discovery is an extremely important part of the publishing cycle. Librarians, bookstore owners, and readers cannot acquire materials that they don't know exist. Cataloging and other metadata play a key role in helping all these groups find publications. (In the following discussion, the term *cataloging* also includes other metadata since cataloging has been the traditional way libraries deal with bibliographic control.) Finding a known item is the least difficult task as long as the searcher has enough bibliographic information about a title, which can now be only a few words. The availability of keyword searching has eliminated the need for the perfect citation required in the print age. For known-item self-published materials, querying Amazon, WorldCat, Goodreads, Smashwords, AddAll, and similar bibliographic databases or even searching with Google (arguably the most comprehensive search engine) should be able to find the item. If these strategies don't work, the item might as well not exist since no practical way exists to get a copy.

Cataloging becomes more important when the searcher wants to expand a search to discover items of potential interest. Traditional library records including both bibliographic and authority files can do, at least in principle, all the following things:

- Find all items where an author has some sort of responsibility
- Identify variant forms of the author's name and any pseudonyms
- Discover coauthors whose works may also be of interest
- Identify title changes, variant forms of the title, and the title in foreign languages
- Determine other items in a series or set whether by the same author or different authors
- Find publications connected with a conference even when the conference changes name or location
- Find all items published by a specific publisher, in a specific location, or even during a specific date range

All these characteristics are reasonably objective and do not depend upon the cataloger's judgment in the way that those in the next section do.

The second set of discovery characteristics deals with the subject content and genre of the work. Keyword searching, while extremely powerful, has its limitations. It does not handle well character strings with radically different meanings. Searching for "mars" can retrieve materials about a Roman god, a planet, a candy bar, and the month of March in French. It also has difficulty with synonyms, regional differences in meaning, and foreign languages. Traditional cataloging and other well-constructed metadata work to solve the problems with these inconsistencies. Even more importantly, traditional cataloging attempts to describe the content through systems like Library of Congress (LC) subject headings, Sears subject headings, and the various systems used in databases, sometimes with the help of their accompanying thesauri. Classification deals with the same issue by grouping similar materials together, often in some sort of hierarchical arrangement. The major classification systems, Library of Congress Classification, the Dewey Decimal Classification, and the Universal Decimal Classifications, are also language independent. In addition, cataloging often identifies the genre of fictional works. Traditional cataloging, as imperfect as it may be, provides access to traditionally published works that is often lacking for self-published materials. A discussion of ways in which potential readers can discover self-published works appears later in this chapter, but one nonbibliographic tool should be noted here that is effective for finding both trade and self-published books, namely, the feature in Amazon, "What Other Items Do Customers Buy after Viewing This Item?" This creative innovation depends upon the collective behavior of Amazon buyers and not on any efforts at bibliographic control.

The second goal of bibliographic control is to control the item as it wends its way through the various steps in the publication, distribution, and use cycle. The various elements described above all play an important role at times; but one feature not yet discussed is critical for the effective management of books, that is, the International Standard Book Number (ISBN). The ISBN was designed to serve as a unique identifier for a specific manifestation of any title and to distinguish among multiple editions and multiple formats. Gordon Foster developed the 9-digit Standard Book Number in 1965. The United States adopted the modified 10-digit ISBN in 1974. In 2007, the ISBN expanded to 13 digits while still maintaining compatibility with the earlier versions ("International Standard Book Number," 2015).

The ISBN, normally acquired by the publisher or author, is assigned in the United States by R. R. Bower (Bowker). With its goal of providing a unique identifier for each manifestation of the work, the ISBN could, at least in principle, be used to control the item without any additional bibliographic information. Since the ISBN is often represented as a bar code, scanners can automatically read the ISBN for tracking purposes. As a unique identifier, the ISBN allows publishers, library jobbers, librarians, and out-of-print vendors to identify and track a book. Similarly, the ISBN provides the most efficient way to search bibliographic files of all types to find a known item among all the possibilities presented by the other types of information such as author, title, and series. In fact, the ISBN may be the only effective way to discover information about bibliographically complex works such as the Bible and works by Shakespeare.

For libraries, bibliographic control is especially important because they need bibliographic records that are as complete as possible in their online finding tools for both user access and internal functions. Libraries expect to acquire these bibliographic records as cheaply as possible as part of the book's purchase price. If the library has to create a record for an item, called original cataloging, this greatly increases the amount of staff time needed even for a brief record. An accurate cost for original cataloging is difficult to determine; but PrairieCat Support, part of a consortium of 127 libraries in Illinois, charges $10 per record for basic original cataloging of standard materials (PrairieCat). A much older article by George D. Harris gave the cost of original cataloging to be as high as $32 but cautioned that cataloging costs mean something different to each library (Harris, 1989). The MARC format was created in the 1960s explicitly to share bibliographic records among libraries, bookstores, and other bibliographic agencies as a way to cut costs (Avram, 2009). OCLC and then later RLG were formed to make cataloging more economical by sharing records created by their members through their extensive online databases. Today, all but the largest libraries can easily acquire most bibliographic records for trade publications from bibliographic utilities like OCLC or from vendors who provide them electronically when the book is ordered or received. One last possibility, mostly for very small libraries, is for libraries to transcribe the cataloging found in the book since most trade publishers include this cataloging from the Library of Congress Cataloging in Publication (CIP) program.

SELF-PUBLISHED MATERIALS AND BIBLIOGRAPHIC CONTROL

The lack of bibliographic control for self-published materials is one of the key obstacles standing in the way of broader library discovery and purchase of self-published books. For American libraries, cataloging records produced by the Library of Congress are considered the best and serve as the gold standard for bibliographic control that other catalog record producers should take as their model. Library of Congress produces these records at several levels, but the full records that most small to mid-size libraries are accustomed to using offer a broad range of information including authors, titles, series, subject headings, and the classification number of the Library of Congress Classification and often the Dewey Decimal Classification. Some records include alternate call numbers and special subject headings for children. LC distributes these records in machine-readable formats relatively inexpensively. The 2015 subscription price for an estimated 238,000 new records was $19,155; the complete retrospective file of 12,668,850 records costs only $27,750 (Library of Congress, Cataloging Distribution Service, 2015). Since these records are not copyrighted for use within the United States, they can then be redistributed without charge (Library of Congress, Cataloging Distribution Service).

Publishers, book vendors, database providers, bibliographic utilities, and integrated library system companies have sophisticated software to manipulate these records. As stated above, many book vendors provide these MARC records to libraries at no or little cost when libraries purchase materials from them; or libraries can acquire them at a minimal cost from the OCLC bibliographic database and other sources.

The Library of Congress has two major streams for creating bibliographic records—the Cataloging in Publication program for mainstream American imprints and the results of its cataloging items for its own collection. Both streams mostly or completely exclude self-published materials, a fact that greatly hinders their discoverability and decreases their desirability for libraries. CIP explicitly excludes self-published materials because they are not from a recognized publisher ("Making cataloging hum," 1996). In a similar fashion, LC does not collect many self-published materials for its collection because they remain tainted by the past history of vanity presses. The information section on LC Card Numbers specifically states: "Please note that many collection policy statements explicitly treat the selection of self-published and vanity press materials." For example, the LC policy for Literature and Language states: "Vanity press and self-published works are not collected, although self-published works of quality may be collected in areas where self-publishing is an important part of the publishing spectrum (e.g., poetry, African American literature)." LC does collect self-published materials in areas such as genealogy where self-publishing has more importance (Library of Congress, Cataloging and Acquisitions).

Libraries and vendors also catalog their own materials and provide the second best way for self-published materials to achieve relatively good bibliographic control. Vendors need these records to control the items and offer them for sale to their customers with the secondary benefit of having a record to share with the library. When cataloging records are not available from other sources, libraries create them or have the records created for them for their integrated library systems. These records make publications available to their patrons and facilitate internal tasks such as circulation, interlibrary loan, and collection analysis. Most often, both vendors and libraries share these records by adding them to one or more of the major bibliographic databases maintained by the bibliographic utilities such as OCLC and SkyRiver. Both libraries and vendors almost always create briefer records than those provided by LC, but they are usually of sufficient quality to meet the needs of libraries without significant editing. Nonetheless, the records created by vendors and publishers provide access to only a small percentage of self-published books. The chapters in this volume by Nardini and Cutler provide additional details on vendor support including cataloging as do the chapters by Bankhead and by DeWild and Jarema on their public library pilot projects.

The most exciting news for improved bibliographic control of self-published works is the cooperative arrangement between Smashwords and OverDrive to sell packages of e-books as well as individual e-books to libraries. According to the press release, this initiative will "bring 200,000+ indie ebooks to 20,000+ public libraries" (Smashwords, 2014). This development is important first because OverDrive is the dominant player in selling e-books to public libraries and has the goal of achieving the same status with school libraries and international libraries. To quote a column from Forbes.com:

> OverDrive dominates the US public library market with its digital platform. . . . In terms of market share, OverDrive says that they serve over 90% of the 16,400 US public libraries, with a 99% renewal rate in that segment. Although right now, they serve somewhat less than 6,000 schools; ultimately, they hope to serve an equally impressive share of the 98,000 school libraries in the U.S. Internationally, the company reports it is doing business with 27,000 schools and libraries. (Seave)

Even more importantly for this chapter, OverDrive states: "When you buy MARC records with OverDrive eBooks you never pay for original cataloging, and holdings are set in WorldCat" (OverDrive). To answer concerns about whether this same policy applies to self-published materials from Smashwords, David Burleigh, director of marketing and communication at OverDrive, confirmed in an e-mail: "Yes, Smashwords titles are treated the same as other titles when it comes to MARC records. We work with OCLC and eBibliofile which provide full MARC records for a small fee, and OverDrive also provides a minimum bib record for free" (Burleigh, personal communication, Junuary 22, 2015). This partnership should create bibliographic records, available in OCLC, for thousands of the most popular self-published books.

Other sources provide partial bibliographic control for self-published materials and, by facilitating the discovery of these items, may eventually lead to more complete bibliographic records if libraries acquire the items. Book reviews, especially those produced by sources intended for libraries, satisfy the discovery function of bibliographic control and often provide reasonably complete information to create at least a minimum-level catalog record. The chapter by Eleanor Cook in this volume discusses book reviewing sources for self-published materials. Her conclusion is that self-published materials are receiving an increasing number of reviews but that the coverage is normally limited to the most popular titles.

The online bookselling sites are also important sources for information. The most comprehensive source for books is Amazon. From the author's personal searching, Amazon includes at least 15,000,000 ranked titles that have sold at least one copy plus many others that have never been bought. Amazon provides basic bibliographic information including publisher, format, language, ISBN, and other details depending upon the record. The advanced search function makes it possible to search in broad subject categories. With a known item, the "what others bought" function as described above can be useful to find related materials. It is important, however, to note here that Amazon does not segregate self-published books from the much larger category of traditional publications. Furthermore, independent sellers, responsible for an estimated 40% of all content on Amazon, often create minimal records that are much less useful for both discovery and cataloging (Loten & Janofsky, 2015).

More useful for bibliographic control are the sites dedicated to helping authors create self-published materials and then distribute them. Smashwords is the most important site because of its efforts to work with libraries including offering packages and individual e-books on OverDrive as described earlier (Smashwords, 2014). In addition, Smashwords sells directly to libraries that purchase larger collections and have the necessary technology to provide digital rights management. Beyond the traditional cataloging records from OverDrive, the records on the Smashwords site normally include the category, publication date, ISBN, and subject tags. Since the authors provide these tags, their ability to accurately describe the content in terms that users, including libraries, use to search may be limited. Brief test searches reveal that any search term must include all the words in the tag to find the item. This makes discovery more difficult because some authors use longer phrases that the average searcher would not consider. On the plus side, it is possible to search tags and other data elements with Boolean operators. Finally, it is possible to use Google to search within tags, a feature that the Smashwords site does not support. These tags would have some use for cataloging by providing suggestions for subject headings or library-supplied metadata. Lulu, the second largest self-publishing site, provides similar information including ISBN, copyright holder, edition, publisher, publication date, pages, binding, and keywords.

One last source for information about self-published materials is the *Books in Print* database that provides entries with basic information such as author, publisher, format, publication date, price, and, of course, the ISBN. As stated above, the ISBN is more useful for control of materials than for the discovery of unknown items. R. R. Bowker is the only agency in the United States that assigns ISBNs, a fact that allows the company to produce

Books in Print. Bowker also uses its databases to gather statistics on publishing, including the number of self-published materials reported above. Nonetheless, their number is underreported since no mandate requires a publication to have an ISBN. Unfortunately, Bowker also does not automatically include all self-published materials with an ISBN in its online *Books in Print* database. The author "must submit . . . meta-data to Bowker on an Advanced Book Information (ABI) form" (Berinstein, 2007) and "register as a publisher" (Bowker Link). The two-step process of first registering as a publisher and then filling out a form for the individual item most likely discourages self-published authors from including their items in this source. Many of the support services for self-publishers include assigning an ISBN as part of their fee.

THE FUTURE

The future for self-published items can only improve with the increasing prominence of self-published materials and the pressure upon libraries to acquire them. The chapters in this volume give evidence of the importance of self-published materials for public libraries but less so for academic libraries. Libraries will need to be motivated to find ways to discover, acquire, and catalog these items; but the popularity of prolific authors as described by Washington in her chapter puts pressure upon public libraries to meet patron demand. As the body of bibliographic information increases, additional libraries will find it easier to make use of existing records and build upon prior efforts. Smashwords' efforts to sell to libraries through OverDrive offer the greatest hope for increased purchasing and subsequent bibliographic control of self-published books. Their preselected packages of the most popular self-published books at a very reasonable cost should lead to the availability of an increased number of acceptable cataloging records.

David Vinjamuri, who teaches branding and social media at NYU and for ThirdWay Brand Trainers, proposes another strategy. A column in his blog on the *Forbes* Web site proposes a solution that hearkens back to many earlier library cooperative ventures. "It would be easy to ignore these [self-published] books if they resembled the vanity press works of previous years. Some do, but others do not. *Publisher's Weekly* [*sic*] estimates that fifteen of the 100 bestselling books of 2012 were self-published." The problem is discovering the good ones. "Yet if each library discovered just one

122 | Self-Publishing and Collection Development

interesting book a year—and shared that result with other libraries . . . there would be 16,000 interesting books for libraries to review. If we assume that just one in one hundred of those reviewed books are 'great' libraries would still have discovered 160 great new books to recommend to library patrons each year" (Vinjamuri, 2013).

Most if not all libraries will be forced to confront the issue of acquiring self-published materials as their numbers and importance grow. Amazon.com, Smashwords, Lulu Enterprises, and other services to support self-publishing are inspiring an increasing number of authors each year to take the plunge. *Publishers Weekly*'s statistic that 15 of the 100 best sellers in 2012 were self-published shows that public demand exists for these items. At some point, a vendor, library group, or a yet unknown entrepreneur will figure out a way to market self-published materials to libraries and to provide the bibliographic control that libraries, librarians, and their patrons demand.

REFERENCES

Avram, H. D. (2009). Machine readable cataloging (MARC): 1961–1974. *Encyclopedia of Library and Information Sciences* (3rd ed.), pp. 3512–3529). Boca Raton, FL: CRC Press.
Berinstein, P. (2007). Publishing trends. Self-publishing and the book trade, part 1: ISBNs, bar codes, and other identifiers. *Searcher, 15*(2), 36.
Bowker. (2014). Get your ISBN today. Retrieved from https://www.myidentifiers.com/Get-your-isbn-now
Bowker. (2013). Self publishing in the United States, 2007–2012. Retrieved from http://media.bowker.com/documents/selfpublishingpubcounts_2007_2012.pdf
Bowker Link, P. A. S. (n.d.). Add/update listings: Frequently asked questions. Retrieved from http://www.bowkerlink.com/corrections/Common/LearnMore.asp
Harris, G. D. (1989). Historic cataloging costs, issues, and trends. *Library Quarterly, 59*, 1–21. http://dx.doi.org/10.1086/602079
International Standard Book Number. (2015). *Wikipedia*. Retrieved from https://en.wikipedia.org/wiki/International_Standard_Book_Number
Library of Congress. (n.d.). Cataloging and acquisitions. Collecting levels. Retrieved from http://www.loc.gov/acq/devpol/cpc.html
Library of Congress. (n.d.). Cataloging distribution service. MARC distribution services ordering instructions. Retrieved from http://www.loc.gov/cds/mdsftp.html

Library of Congress. (2015). Cataloging distribution service. 2015 MDS record counts and prices. Retrieved from http://loc.gov/cds/PDFdownloads/mds2015.pdf

Loten, A., & Janofsky, A. (2015). Sellers need Amazon, but at what cost? *Wall Street Journal.*

Making cataloging hum: CIP celebrates 25th anniversary. (1996). *Library of Congress Information Bulletin, 55*, 322–323.

OverDrive. (2004). eBook MARC records save time & money. Retrieved from http://company.overdrive.com/files/DLRMARCAvailable.pdf

PrairieCat. (n.d.). PrairieCat support. Retrieved from https://support.prairiecat.info/services/cataloging

Seave, A. (2013). Are digital libraries a "winner-takes-all" market? OverDrive hopes so. Retrieved from http://www.forbes.com/sites/avaseave/2013/11/18/are-digital-libraries-a-winner-takes-all-market-overdrive-hopes-so/

Smashwords. (2014). Smashwords and OverDrive to bring 200,000+ indie ebooks to 20,000+ public libraries. Retrieved from http://blog.smashwords.com/2014/05/smashwords-and-overdrive-to-bring.html

Vinjamuri, D. (2013). Why public libraries matter: And how they can do more. Retrieved from http://www.forbes.com/sites/davidvinjamuri/2013/01/16/why-public-libraries-matter-and-how-they-can-do-more/

10 | Self-Publishing and Libraries: The Slush Pile Is the Platform

Tom Bruno, Yale University

INTRODUCTION

The intersection of self-publishing and the library world is still very much a moving target. Here we will examine various platforms and models of support for independent and self-published authors and investigate how libraries are contributing to the writing and self-publishing ecosystems, both locally and online through various digital initiatives.

ADVENTURES IN SELF-PUBLISHING: A PERSONAL JOURNEY

I had never intended to set out along the path of self-publication. My writing efforts began long before e-books were a big thing, when Amazon was still a river in South America and the business model of self-publishing involved printing a large stash of physical copies at one's own expense and trying to sell them door to door. After writing all throughout my precocious junior and senior high school years, I found myself somewhat overwhelmed by college, then by the real world, such that, when I did come back to complete my first short story in years, I felt somewhat bewildered by the strange new electronic world that had begun to take hold in creative circles.

Full of enthusiasm and several stories' worth of new material, I briefly considered skipping what I had always thought to be the standard *cursus honorum* for a writer—whereby a short story in a local literary journal translates to a novella somewhere else, then soon requests for an anthology, or perhaps even a book deal for an actual entire novel-length work of fiction—and take my stories directly to the Internet; but, at the time I was pondering such an alternative course of action, the mechanisms for doing so hadn't quite taken hold. No, I was resolved to do things the old-fashioned way—query, submit, rinse, and repeat—until I finally found a willing agent for one of my stories and signed my first "traditional" publishing contract.

My writing piqued some editors' interest; and a couple of times I was even asked for pages from my fantasy novel, which I had at long last completed; but, aside from getting one of my science fiction short stories published in a short-lived literary zine, I found myself getting discouraged by rejection after rejection . . . after rejection. This is, of course, nothing new to an aspiring writer. In fact, almost every successful author cautions would-be wordsmiths that they will likely find themselves staring at rejection slips, letters, and e-mails hundreds if not thousands of times before their big break finally arrives—and that's assuming that a prospective editor or agent even answers at all.

TOO MANY WRITERS OR A PARADIGM SHIFT WAITING TO HAPPEN?

Getting past the gatekeepers of the traditional publishing world was always envisioned as a protracted siege, but something happened along the way that made this journeyman period seem less and less like a required step on the path toward becoming a professional writer and more and more a completely hopeless prospect. At least, this is what it felt like to me and countless other authors. What was interesting (at least to me) was that this growing frustration and impatience with the traditional path of publication seemed to predate the self-publishing revolution.

Had the personal computing revolution unleashed a surge of young new writers who eschewed the cumbersome technology of typewriters and white-out for their word processors? Had Stephen King unwittingly produced a legion of storytelling acolytes with his seminal book *On Writing*, which demystified the craft of writing to a generation, much to the delight of many who found Mr. King's books a welcome antidote for the aspiring nonliterary author . . . as well as arousing the horror of many others who found themselves competing with a fresh crop of writers? Or was it National Novel Writing Month, which loosed a torrent of new manuscripts onto the slush piles of many a publishing house every December following a month-long orgy of unnecessary exposition, bloated word counts, and adverbs—so many adverbs, as far as the eye could see?

THE SLUSH PILE VS. THE LONG TAIL

Whatever it was, I couldn't help but notice fellow authors begin to lose faith in being able to slip past the gatekeepers as their illustrious predecessors did before them. Authors started posting their stories online for free—be it on their blogs, linked as documents to their own personal Web sites, or what have you. Better to put one's writing out there and share it with those who might find it enjoyable rather than consign it to a slush pile where it would remain silent and unread for as long as it laid there. This, it seems to me now only in retrospect, was the beginning of the sea change. The atmosphere of vexation at the traditional methods of publication was being stoked by the digital revolution even before the now-established platforms for self-publication had evolved.

Was this simply narcissism on our generation's part, an *American Idol* sense of entitlement, which fueled our frustration and made us feel that our creative output deserved to be distributed to the public, even if it couldn't pass the muster of the literary Powers That Be? Perhaps. I'm not afraid to own up to a portion of this charge; but, at the same time, I think the emerging concept of the long tail and the related ability to utilize the Internet to appeal to a smaller and more targeted niche market truly did change the equation for many of us, such that, when Amazon, Smashwords, and other platforms for self-publication became available, there was a critical mass of authors out there who were just disenchanted enough with the traditional publishing scene that taking the self-publishing plunge no longer seemed to be an act of artistic suicide.

KINDLE DIRECT PUBLISHING

So having been unsuccessful in finding an agent interested in my manuscript—a fantasy novel about the coming of age of an itinerant chef—after publishing it chapter by chapter on my own personal blog, I decided to give it one final editorial pass and upload it through the Kindle Direct Publishing portal, where I could offer it for sale as an e-book. The initial publication was something of a dud, with only a few friends buying a copy; but then Amazon came up with a master stroke for its Kindle Direct Publishing platform—the ability to offer free promotions for your e-books for several days during a given period. A successfully managed promotion could enable an author to rocket up into the bestselling lists for e-books, garnering extra attention and hopefully securing enough favorable reviews so that, when the book did return to its normal price, one would enjoy a healthy sales "bump" afterwards. While the efficacy of these promotions has certainly faltered over time, for many authors this meant the difference between sharing our books with a small circle of family and friends and getting them noticed by a broader circle of readers.

To be sure, there is a certain amount of both showmanship and gamesmanship involved in a successful self-publication career. One must not only take advantage of multiple promotional channels, either via social media or other free or paid advertising methods, but one must also craft one's literary portfolio in as strategic a manner as possible. For example, self-published authors need to use the right combination of edited content, carefully chosen keywords, at least passable cover art, and description copy to entice their readers; at the same time, for the best possible commercial results, they need to write and publish a steady enough stream of new fiction to keep readers engaged and hungry for more. Too many would-be self-published authors—myself included—will release a book or two and simply wait too long before releasing the next installment in the series, thereby losing a potential second, third, or subsequent sale from a reader who has already moved on to "binge-read" a different author.

The most successful self-published authors swear by their own formulas for targeting fiction markets, producing new content, and releasing it in a manner that is optimized for the best exposure, reviews, and sales. A few of these writers find that, as a result, their sales and greater recognition open doors in the traditional publishing world that had hitherto remained closed or had not even revealed themselves at all—some of these authors will forego self-publishing altogether while others will continue to pursue selling on their own platform or with some blended version of the two modes of publication. Far many more other self-published authors, however, will never enjoy this "breakout" moment through publishing their content online. To be fair, most self-published authors are content with simply making their writing available and accessible to a wider audience and aren't necessarily trying to make a living through or retire on their self-publishing paycheck. I for one wouldn't say I don't occasionally check my statistics at Kindle Direct Publishing and hope that someone decided to single me out as a literary genius and undiscovered talent, but in the meantime I am mindful that hundreds if not thousands of people have read and enjoyed my writing already.

This is particularly the case when writing highly targeted genre fiction. For example, over the past year or two, I have been working on a science fiction anthology featuring libraries and librarians titled "L Is for Librarian." While I have tried to write these stories in a manner that may appeal to the layperson reader or general science fiction enthusiast, the issues and themes explored in this series are of primary appeal to people who currently work in a library setting or are practitioners of library science. Realistically speaking, what is the largest potential audience for such a genre within a genre— that is, what is the subset of science fiction fans who are also librarians or librarians who are also science fiction fans? While writing for such a limited market may seem at first to be stifling, in fact I have found my experience to be the exact opposite as my efforts to write, edit, publish, and market this series have been met with great enthusiasm and encouragement from my librarian colleagues as well as offers of additional writing opportunities and other collaborative proposals, which have emerged from this effort.

1,000 TRUE FANS AND SELF-PUBLISHING

The notion of writing for a smaller audience is not an altogether new one. In a 2008 blog post, former *Wired* editor Kevin Kelly famously declared that an artist only needed "1,000 True Fans" in order to make a living in the new creative world of digital discovery and distribution:

> A True Fan is defined as someone who will purchase anything and everything you produce. They will drive 200 miles to see you sing. They will buy the super deluxe re-issued hi-res box set of your stuff even though they have the low-res version. They have a Google Alert set for your name. They bookmark the eBay page where your out-of-print editions show up. They come to your openings. They have you sign their copies. They buy the t-shirt, and the mug, and the hat. They can't wait till you issue your next work. They are true fans. (http://kk.org/thetechnium/2008/03/1000-true-fans/)

Over the years, Kelly's provocative thesis has been debated by both struggling artists and wags in the various creative industries; during this time singers, writers, and others have tried to make a living through self-publishing and direct engagement with their fans. Some have become "microcelebrities" to their established niche markets. One musician and songwriter, Robert Rich, spoke with Kevin Kelly on his blog to describe his own experience with creating music as a microcelebrity:

> The sort of artist who survives at the long tail is the sort who would be happy doing nothing else, who willingly sacrifices security and comfort for the chance to communicate something meaningful, hoping to catch the attention of those few in the world who seek what they also find meaningful. It's a somewhat solitary existence, a bit like a lighthouse keeper throwing a beam out into the darkness, in faith that this action might help someone unseen.

> In reality the life of a "microcelebrity" resembles more the fate of Sisyphus, whose boulder rolls back down the mountain every time he reaches the summit. After every tour I feel exhausted but empowered by the thought that a few people really care a lot about this music. Yet, a few months later all is quiet again and CD/download sales slow down again. If I take the time to concentrate for a year on what I hope to be a breakthrough album, that time of silence widens out into a gaping hole and interest seems to fade. When I finally do release something that I feel to be a bold new direction, I manage only to sell it to the same 1,000 True Fans. The boulder sits back at the bottom of the mountain and it's time to start rolling it up again. (http://kk.org/thetechnium/2008/04/the-reality-of/)

KICKSTARTER AS AN ALTERNATIVE TO TRADITIONAL PUBLISHING

The fascinating coda to this debate has been the rise of Kickstarter and other online platforms for crowdsourcing the funding of creative endeavors. Whereas the self-published artist would originally need to engage his or her readers/listeners/consumers with direct sales or some kind of subscription model, the Kickstarter movement allowed independent creators instead to seek investors to underwrite their creative ambitions from start to finish, in effect substituting their support for the capital that traditional publishing would outlay on behalf of a newly signed writer. This money would then go in turn to hire editors, designers, and all of the other pre- and post-production bells and whistles that the artists seeking support felt were necessary for the successful completion of their projects. On their blog, Kickstarter's founders write:

> We started Kickstarter as a new way for creators and audiences to work together to make things. The traditional funding systems are risk-averse and profit-focused, and tons of great ideas never get a chance as a result. We thought Kickstarter could open the door to a much wider variety of ideas and allow everyone to decide what they wanted to see exist in the world. Kickstarter is full of ambitious, innovative, and imaginative ideas that aren't possible anywhere else. (https://www.kickstarter.com/blog/accountability-on-kickstarter)

What Kickstarter has done is co-opted the notion of 1,000 True Fans and made the relationship between a creator and a fan less discrete and more of a patron or donor model.

PATREON AND THE PATRON-SUBSCRIPTION MODEL OF SELF-PUBLISHING

The success of such a new funding paradigm for creative endeavors has led to a proliferation of similar platforms; some of them, such as Patreon, are more targeted toward the indie artist community. Patreon represents a blended model between the project-based funding platform of Kickstarter and the direct sales scheme powered by Amazon and other online marketplaces supporting self-publication. Instead of asking for donations toward a single funding campaign (like Kickstarter) or advertising new works for sale, the Patreon author asks backers to pledge their financial support either on a monthly or per-work basis. Independent musicians have flocked to Patreon since the platform's launch as has the gaming community, which has found itself progressively disenchanted with supporting larger and more ambitious Kickstarter projects in hopes of a getting a playable product for their pledges. Writers are beginning to discover the utility of the Patreon model of self-publication as well:

> Cara Ellison always felt like something was missing. Although the Scottish videogame critic was an established writer at multiple websites and magazines about games, she had long tired

of superficial press junkets and canned press releases. She wanted to do the sort of long-form, embedded journalism with game creators that she saw in music and film, to spend days or even weeks with the creators she thought were making fascinating, important games—even if they weren't big-budget, mainstream titles—and dig into what made those people tick.

The problem was, no one wanted to run it.

"There was just no place for it," says Ellison. It was the sort of writing that always seemed to slip between the cracks: Most video game websites didn't have the time or money to fund it, while most mainstream publications with bigger budgets saw it as niche content. Still, she felt that there was at least a boutique audience that was hungry for this sort of reporting—and willing to pay for it, even if editors weren't. So she turned to a crowdfunding service that she thought would be uniquely helpful for her work: Patreon. (http://www.wired .com/2014/05/patreon/)

LIBRARY PUBLISHING TOOLKIT, WRITING GROUPS, AND LOCAL AUTHOR EVENTS

Libraries can serve a similar role as patrons to self-published authors. In the *Library Publishing Toolkit*, editor Allison Brown highlights several library systems that have taken an active role in aiding and encouraging local aspiring writers. "I noticed two common denominators when I spoke to libraries about their thriving writing communities: clever use of space and enthusiastic participants. Before talking about publishing print-on-demand titles, acquiring an Espresso Book Machine, or offering e-book publishing courses, libraries should be playing a role in supporting the writing process" (Brown & Oberlander, 2013). The reasons for doing so are not entirely altruistic. By imbricating ourselves into the world of self-publication, Brown argues, libraries can help enforce standards for description and discovery as well as foster some critical and editorial oversight by means of such things as writing circles, local author days, and even workshops taught by members of the writing community.

For example, the Princeton Public Library in Princeton, New Jersey, began supporting self-published authors by offering a quiet space for writers participating in the NaNoWriMo contest every November. The library also offers space to several different writing groups and hosts a Local Authors' Day featuring both local and independent writers. In Bay City, Michigan, the Wirt Public Library organizes a Writers' Night, inviting both traditionally published and self-published authors to speak about their own writing and publication processes. The Safety Harbor Public Library in Safety Harbor, Florida, helps support its enclave of local artists with several writers' circles for poets and other authors as well as offering instruction in how to use the library as a tool for researching, writing, and even publication. Library staff have held informational sessions on how to self-publish books on different platforms, including crowdsourcing support platforms such as Kickstarter.

A RADICAL PROPOSITION: THE AUTHOR INCUBATOR PROGRAM

The Douglas County Library System in Colorado aims to take this support to a completely different level of involvement with what it calls its Author Incubator Program. An offshoot of its innovative and successful e-book lending program, the Author Incubator would help provide the broadest range of e-content to their patrons by co-opting these same patrons as part of the content creation process as well as other independent and self-published authors. Douglas County librarians, therefore, would not simply be in the business of instructing the community in their use of the library's resources in order to assist them in the writing and publishing process but would also help library patrons discover and access this e-content that they helped produce in the first place. Once an author has self-published his or her work on a platform such as Smashwords, the book would then be vetted by a group of volunteer "citizen acquisition editors," who would follow established guidelines for editing and content to add the book to the library catalog; the book would also be rated and reviewed by a member of the volunteer cataloging committee, which helps make it more discoverable.

So when will this Author Incubator Program make its debut? Douglas County Library System's James LaRue is confident that they will be able to launch in some capacity in the near future. For other libraries contemplating adopting a similar role with their local writing community, LaRue outlines the following structural prerequisites:

1. Establish a technical infrastructure. There are at least three approaches. First, a library might choose some vendor to host and enable the discovery of local content (Autographics has announced such a project). But do we need a middleman? Second, a library might choose to invest in its own hardware, software, and telecommunications capacity to do that. This is the Douglas County model, which is up and running, and Queens (N.Y.) Public Library is launching its own version of this. Third, libraries might team up to invest in such a setup together. This is what the consortium Marmot has done in Colorado, and Califa has done in California. For libraries that already operate their own servers and networks, this is a significant but not prohibitively expensive task. For libraries starting from scratch, the assistance of state libraries and federal grants may be necessary. In any case, I think this phase is the work of at least a year.

2. Build new systems of publisher relations, acquisitions, and workflow. DCL has contracted for the development of an acquisition system to better integrate the compilation of catalogs from mid-list, independent, and small publishers not currently carried by our distributors. We're beta testing it. When it's complete, we hope other libraries will adopt it. We are eager to share all the data we have already harvested or created. But working directly with publishers is different than working through a distributor. It requires the thoughtful reconsideration of many longstanding processes. It's fair to say that this deconstruction and reconstruction of workflow is worth a year in itself. But some of it may run parallel with the first phase.

3. Manage demand. To date, libraries mostly respond to demand, and that demand is dictated by the advertising budgets of the Big Six. But it seems clear that the annual output of new titles by independent and self-publishers is already at least twice that of mainstream commercial publishing. If libraries want to stay in the game of sampling the intellectual content of our times, we have to find a way to acquire far more than our current budgets allow. I believe what's likely to work is a combination of the process I outlined above with a broad outreach to the small and independent publishers eager to work with us. (http://www.americanlibrariesmagazine.org/article/wanna-write-good-one-library-publisher)

BIBLIOBOARD AND SELF-E

Library Journal recently tossed its hat into the self-publishing ring as well by partnering with the e-content aggregator and vendor BiblioBoard to offer SELF-e, a discovery service that connects self-published authors with library patrons. "Using SELF-e, authors can submit their self-published ebook(s) directly, and LJ will evaluate and select promising works for inclusion in curated collections sorted by genre that participating public libraries can make available to their patrons all over the United States. In addition, authors can opt in to include their ebook(s) in statewide collections with other local authors, whether or not they are selected for LJ's genre collections" (http://www.slj.com/2014/05/books-media/ebooks/library-journal-launches-self-publishing-partnership-with-biblioboard/).

Self-published authors can participate in SELF-e by submitting their e-book file and granting a nonexclusive license to make their book available to public library patrons via subscribing institutions in the public library market, including subscribing public libraries in the author's state. Books that pass through the curation process for SELF-e will become discoverable and downloadable content through the platform with authors receiving a promotional badge they can use when advertising their e-books on other retail outlets. Even if an author's self-published book is not selected by curators for wider distribution by the SELF-e program, it can still be included in that author's SELF-e (noncurated) state module with other local and self-published authors.

SELFPUBLISHEDAUTHOR BY BOWKER
AND MARKETING TO LIBRARIES

ProQuest affiliate Bowker has also launched its own platform for assisting and supporting independent writers—SelfPublishedAuthor.com is a Web resource for self-publishing by offering how-to guides, advice, and even webinars via a series of a thematic blogs in order to guide authors through the basics of producing their own quality e-content. "Bowker has tracked extraordinary growth in the number of self-published works over the past five years," said Beat Barblan, Bowker director of identifier services. "There are thousands of authors who need access to advice, guidance and resources. SelfPublishedAuthor.com is designed to be their partner, helping them bring their books to market in the most effective way" (http://www.bowker.com/en-US/aboutus/press_room/2013/pr_05202013.shtml).

One of the topics addressed by this resource is how to get self-published books and e-books into libraries. In a publishing world where brick-and-mortar bookstores are increasingly disappearing from the consumer landscape, libraries continue to represent a viable emerging market for independent and self-published authors. Due to time and budget constraints, however, as well as legacy collection development infrastructures that emphasize the discovery and purchase of traditionally published library materials, librarians are often both ill-equipped and ill-advised to navigate this overwhelming new market, even if the material therein would prove to be more interesting and/or relevant to their local library patrons' reading or research interests. At a 2014 uPublishU conference for independent and self-published authors in New York City, Ian Singer, vice president and group publisher at Library Journals, announced that a survey of library users revealed that "60 to 70 per cent of patrons want self-published titles to be available in their libraries" (http://lj.libraryjournal.com/2014/06/industry-news/self-published-authors-learn-to-market-to-libraries/).

BEST LIBRARY PRACTICES FOR SELF-PUBLISHED AUTHORS

Nevertheless, the lack of standards for formatting and describing self-published content also provides a natural roadblock for librarians who would otherwise consider adding independent and self-published authors to their library collections. To address this problem, Laura Carruba, assistant cataloger at the Roanoke County Public Library, offers some practical guidelines for independent and self-published authors who wish to create e-content that is easy for libraries to discover, acquire, and (of course) catalog (http://ideatrash.net/2014/01/how-to-make-life-easy-for-librarians-so.html).

1. Create a title page, both front and back. If your publisher of choice charges by the page or by the gathering (a group of folded sheets sewn or glued into a book's binding), spend the extra money to add this crucial page. Use the other pages to add an "about the author" page to your book, or endpapers with maps, or advertise other books you've self-published.
2. Give the following information on your title page and/or verso:
    *   Author name
    *   Place of publication
    *   Publisher (if you created a publishing LLC, or the author name if you didn't)
    *   Copyright date (and print date if the two dates are different)

3. If you publish under a pseudonym, including your real name on the verso is a big help. Many authors with famous pseudonyms, such as J. D. Robb for Nora Roberts, have cross-references in the LCSH so someone can find all the works by one person using multiple names.

4. If your work is a multi-chapter novel or collection of short stories or poems, consider adding a table of contents. Microsoft Word and Open/LibreOffice include tutorials on how to create them and update them with new content in case you created a ToC with a draft of your work.

5. Number your pages. MS Word and open-source variants include instructions on how to do this as well.

6. Write a back cover blurb that talks about what you wrote, and try not to compare it to other books, movies, TV shows, etc. If you have a press package or pitch letter, chances are you've already tried to describe your book. Find a good paragraph from one of those sources and use that.

7. Purchase an International Standard Book Number (ISBN) from Bowker. (They are at https://www.myidentifiers.com/.) From a library viewpoint, an ISBN provides a measure of professionalism. From a cataloger viewpoint, it's a clue leading to distinct information about the author, the title, and the individual volume of dead tree pulp needing a catalog record. For authors, as Steve says in this blog post, an independent ISBN from Bowker allows an author to sell in multiple online venues.

CONCLUSION: BEYOND THE SLUSH PILE

This all-too-brief survey of the various points of contact between self-publishing and the library is no doubt colored by my own personal experiences as a would-be independent author. To be fair, for every experiment in supporting local self-published and independent authors that I have attempted to illuminate in this chapter, there are doubtless myriad other examples of successful and unsuccessful attempts to do the same found elsewhere. My own list was therefore not meant to be exhaustive but as a jumping-off point for one's own investigations into the world of self-publishing. However, what I do think this survey highlights is that there is still no one dominant paradigm for how the library world will ultimately make sense of the problem of patron-created content. If libraries are still wrestling only with the consequences of a world where the preponderance of library materials are digital, it is incumbent on librarians to begin to think about how they will collect, curate, and support a future library ecosystem of independent and self-published authors, as this future has already arrived.

REFERENCE

Brown, A., & Oberlander, C. (Eds.). (2013). *Library publishing toolkit*. Geneseo, NY: IDS Project Press.

11 | An Indie Author in a Library World

AlTonya Washington, Livingstone College

I've been fortunate to sit on both sides of the publishing spectrum. Traditionally, I've gained a loyal and happy following of readers who enjoy my historical and contemporary romances. These satisfied readers have supported me throughout my career—even when that career took me into the world of independent publishing. When all is said and done, readers only care about one name on the book—the author's. Sadly, this train of thought does not seem to hold true in the library realm, which has only seemed to value works created only in the traditional publishing world.

I'm often asked why I decided to venture into the world of self-publishing when I was blessed enough to acquire a book deal from an internationally known publishing house. Quite simply, it was my readers who made this leap not only a successful one, but a necessary one. The rejection of my fourth title in my then three-book series chronicling the Ramsey family out of Seattle, Washington, set me on my journey of becoming an independent publisher. The publishing house still loved my voice and remained interested in publishing my work. My traditional publishers were not, however, interested in more stories in this series (which has been spun off to include another family and, as of November 2014, stands at 18 popular titles thanks to my insatiable readers).

In 2009, my career forked off toward the independent publishing world. My only concern then was continuing the unfinished series for my readers. I didn't stop to think (or even care to think) about how this independently published work would be received in the library world. I should probably have given it a little more thought as, once the work was completed, it would need to be made available, right? Even now, years later, I can't say that, if I had it all to do again, I would have put greater effort into finding a new traditional publisher for the work. I had the opportunity back then to do just that. A few well-known houses were interested in the work, but something about sheltering the Ramsey family under the roof of a new house just didn't sit right with me. I knew that the plot I was building for this crew would not play nicely with certain publishing guidelines that I was already familiar with. It went without saying that publishing with a new house would only bring along more guidelines. I wanted the freedom to create this story as I saw fit, and my readers were all on board with that.

At this time, I had been making my living in the library field for about eight years. I had spent about two and a half years working as a reference associate for a public library before moving on to the academic environment where I spent another eight years working as a library serials assistant for a private college in North Carolina. I was getting a very good education in how libraries worked. Not until I went to work in the technical services department as a serials assistant did I come to understand more about the collection development process. Of course, I've never expected to see work such as mine gracing the shelves of an academic library, or at least not back then. Now, however, academic libraries are appearing to grasp the importance of enhancing their fiction sections with material more likely to interest leisure readers. This strategy is designed to increase library use and is proving highly successful. Still, academic libraries are not flooding their shelves with romance novels or with independently published titles no matter what the subject matter.

Again, this is not surprising. We are talking about academic libraries, after all. Still, working in the academic environment is where I've had the greatest opportunity to see the selection process at work. My day job now consists of helping to build my library's collection where I've worked as a reference librarian for the past two years. Librarians rely on varying resources to assist in that selection process. They attend conferences where they have the chance to visit with book vendors and discuss what direction current reading trends are taking. They subscribe to most respected publications that not only discuss these trends but also review the latest in reading material. Such reviews are often the deciding factor in what librarians will choose to add to their collections. Herein lays a huge roadblock to the indie author seeking library shelf space.

BOOK REVIEWS

Publications such as *Publishers Weekly, Library Journal, Booklist,* and *Kirkus Reviews* are staples for librarians when building collections. Librarians lean heavily on the views presented in these publications when making selection choices. As a traditional author, I've had my titles regularly reviewed in *Romantic Times BOOKClub Magazine,* another well-respected publication that librarians use when building their fiction collections. *Romantic Times* has recently started reviewing independently published titles. Keep in mind that these publications often require a copy of the work at least four months in advance of the publication date. Things can move pretty quickly in the indie world, and setting a release date to accommodate a review can be a stumbling block for the author who plans to make his or her work available as soon as it's completed. As a whole, many indie authors will find that the aforementioned publications and many like them won't even touch a self-published work for review. Within the first few lines of many review submission guidelines, you are likely to see the statement "We Do Not Read Self-Published Work" or something to that effect. This is not to say that indie authors can't break the mold and get their work reviewed, but it's far from easy unless the indie work is gaining a tremendous buzz. Also, indie authors can work on perhaps getting a feature story done that will gain them notice as well.

So why is it so difficult for an independently published author to get work reviewed in such publications? While I'm in no position to give a definitive response, as a librarian weighing this issue, I could say that an indie publication is perhaps not properly vetted the way that traditional material would be. A self-published title may or may not be edited by anyone other than the author. Traditional titles go through several hands before the book even goes into production. An author submits a proposal to the editor who decides whether the idea has merit—usually, in fact, the editor meets with a team of other editors and assistants who weigh in on that decision. If the idea is approved, once the manuscript is written, the author submits it for extensive copyediting on grammar, story structure, and other factors. This should not mean that a traditionally published story is better than an independent one, but it is often the standard by which such stories are measured. This is unfortunate, given that grammatical errors, dry plots, back cover copy discrepancies, and other negatives often exist in abundance amidst the pages of traditionally published works. Since traditional publications have the benefit of being reviewed by more than one set of eyes, there is, however, greater opportunity to catch and correct these faults.

In the years that I've been in the independent publishing game, things have improved. Indie work is garnering a lot more respect than it had in the past. Publishing houses have reached out to well-received self-published authors to re-release those publications on a grander scale. This is a blessing, for any self-published author is all too familiar with the next dreaded obstacle: distribution.

DISTRIBUTION

Whether traditionally or independently published, a book has little hope of being read if a reader can't find it. In spite of the popularity of e-books, having printed books appear on the shelves of libraries across the country is still a dream for many authors. Additionally, there are still readers who prefer holding an actual printed title in their hands. As an independently published author, I've had the chance to see this shift play out over the years. When I published my first indie title in 2009, I worked with a company who pretty much did all the work for me—all I had to do was pay them. It wasn't until I started publishing my books via Amazon's CreateSpace and Kindle platforms that I really got my greatest education in this world of on-demand publishing.

My e-book title *Truth in Sensuality* (March 2009) was published exclusively via the Kindle and CreateSpace platforms. I was one of the first traditionally published African American romance authors to utilize these platforms. Publishing *Truth in Sensuality* was about my breaking free of the traditional publishing molds. I never expected this erotic romance title to wind up on a library's shelves. I wrote it because the subject matter for me was about as far removed from anything I'd done up until that time. This title and the next several books that I published in print and electronically with Amazon's CreateSpace and Kindle platforms also allowed me to witness a shift in other publishing molds as well. I noticed that my print titles did quite well. I'm not an e-book person, but I made the titles available in that format to accommodate all my readers. Gradually, I began to take notice of the sizable shift in sales from print to digital. Many indie authors choose to publish exclusively in e-book format; I can't quite get myself to that way of thinking and continue to release titles electronically and in print. I suppose it's the librarian in me. The topic of print distribution is still relevant to me.

Distribution is vital, especially for the self-published author. Distribution, however, can be even harder to obtain than a book review. For the author looking to have books grace a library's shelves, it is a necessity. Unfortunately, the term "on demand" is what generally seems to freeze distributors in their tracks. Once the library makes its decision on what material it wants to purchase, it usually connects with its distributor to place the order. Although libraries sometimes buy directly, it's most common to use the services of the distributor. Distributors purchase books in bulk and make their money when the client makes its purchases. What happens if the client doesn't make those purchases? Do the books just sit looking pretty in a warehouse? No. The distributor must have a way of returning the product if it cannot be sold. There is a return policy agreement between distributors and publishers. In the on-demand world, once a title is purchased, it's then printed and shipped with no returns.

It's a frustrating situation for any indie author, but it's doubly frustrating for a traditionally published independent author. I watched my traditional titles being preordered by libraries across the country. My independent titles barely got a nod. I recall e-mailing a collection development librarian at a nearby library 20 minutes away from my home. She told me that they would be unable to carry my books in their library and wished me good luck placing my work elsewhere. At that point, the blinders finally began to fall away; I realized it was a distribution thing. It had to be, given the fact that the library was definitely carrying all my traditional titles. In defense of the library, however, it generally comes down to a financial decision. There are far more authors in the world than there are libraries, and libraries are bound by the frustrating word "budgets."

BUDGET

As a librarian and an author, I can identify with the frustrations that exist on both sides. In my own collection development capacities for my library, there is material I would love to acquire for our shelves that we simply cannot afford. Budgetary issues have always held relevance for libraries; but, with the lingering effects of the economic crises, libraries are still reeling from shorter hours, smaller staffs, and decreased funding. What money a library has must be spent wisely, and that means librarians must lean more heavily on their traditional decision making to help them make choices that are both economical and beneficial to their patrons.

For an academic library, this is especially challenging. While we are eager to build our fiction sections to attract more leisure readers and thereby increase our library traffic statistics, the bulk of our funds must be dedicated to building our academic collection. While traditional public libraries aren't so focused on acquiring materials to satisfy various academic disciplines, they too have collection areas that they must work to maintain and keep relevant. Reference materials consist of everything from books to training materials, newspapers, and periodicals. The children's area must hold material that is both entertaining and educational for young readers. Libraries also strive to meet the needs of those who visit their facilities for more than print materials. Film and music offerings as well as materials necessary for history and genealogical research require a large amount of a library's financial resources. I could devote another few pages to discussing the costs of Internet/wireless access and electronic database subscriptions.

So libraries must make their money stretch quite a distance. They purchase a lot more than books. Being selective in the reading materials they add to the collection is as much about adding quality for their readers as it is about being economical in order to provide the necessities that all their users require.

As stated earlier, I can identify with the frustrations that exist on the side of the author as well as the side of the librarian. There are, of course, those librarians that don't need to lean on the reviews of the most renowned publications or be tied down by budgetary restrictions when it comes to avoiding ordering independent materials. These librarians wouldn't place an order for an indie title to save their lives. Some feel that nothing comes out of that pool but rubbish and that authors who independently publish only do so because they couldn't get a traditional contract. When met with the argument that these authors don't earn a lot of money in self-publishing, these librarians say that it must be the authors' massive egos that are the motivating factor.

As an indie author, I can honestly say that some of these viewpoints do have some validity. I've come across some releases that are really disturbing—the titles and story overviews alone are enough to give me a shudder.

I know it's these kinds of works that add fuel to those unfortunate arguments and make it more difficult for the really worthy independently published material to get a true shot at being purchased. As a result, it's not an easy thing (or timely and cost-efficient) for a librarian to successfully wade through subpar material to get to those works that show real promise.

The intention of this chapter is not to dissuade all indie authors, to suggest that they just give up and stop trying to get their work placed in libraries. Libraries are still some of the best places to connect with readers. Any author, traditional or independent, can connect with a library to ask about organizing author events though the answer isn't always positive. Such opportunities often open doorways to getting an author's work more seriously considered for shelf placement. My personal experience in this area has gone remarkably well despite my setbacks. I've had the chance to host reader discussions and take part in author panels and expos at many libraries. Aside from differences in opinion related to what does or does not belong on a library's shelf, librarians have proven to be great supporters of author visits. I realize that a lot of my success has come from the fact that I'm traditionally published. I tend to introduce myself that way by letting the library know that they already have my titles on their shelves. In my experience, readers will most often want to lend a large portion of the discussion to my independent material.

The question still remains, however, how does this all pan out for the independent authors who don't have a traditional writing career following them into the indie publishing world? What chance do they have of getting noticed, of having librarians take them seriously enough to offer shelf placement? Perhaps my answer here may sound a bit naïve, but I've been a published author for more than 11 years. In that time, reading trends have changed; new reading genres have materialized; new reading formats and ways to publish have been invented. Throughout this wealth of change, one thing, for me, has remained constant—the readers.

READERS

Once again, the traditional world has benefited me greatly. I brought with me into the independent market an impressive number of readers that helped make this leap a lot more successful a lot more quickly than it would have been otherwise. As I stated earlier, readers really only care about one name on the cover—the author's. Still, that doesn't mean that authors can or should take their readers for granted. Even in the indie world, rules exist. They exist for those who care about presenting a quality product meant to please readers and enhance their reading experience. Readers who finish an author's work and claim that the experience was an enjoyable one are readers who will return for more of that author's work. They will read that title in print or online. They will bombard the author with questions about the release date for a follow-up work, how the author came up with the idea, and what else the author has written that the reader can enjoy until the aforementioned follow-up work is complete. In short, they want access to that author's work, and that usually means they want it in their libraries.

When all is said and done, librarians and authors—*all* authors—have a common interest—the readers. Librarians strive to stock their shelves with the latest, greatest reads as well as the most revered classics. They want the most popular magazines on the shelves because that's what their readers want; they want the nicest, most durable (and yes, cost-conscious) furniture in place so that their patrons can have a comfortable place to sit. Authors, like libraries, want to provide a great story for the readers. The readers often make this possible when they make suggestions for library purchases.

Readers have a huge amount of influence when it comes to the choice of what a library stocks on its shelves. I often browse WorldCat just to get a glimpse of how my titles—usually my traditional titles—are doing in the library world. It's amazing to see how many of my self-published works are in libraries in places I've never even heard of. I owe such a great deal of that to my readers. Relying on reader suggestions to move your books into libraries may seem like going along at a snail's pace, especially for the independent author who has yet to build a wide-reaching audience; but it is a steady route not to be dismissed.

OTHER AVENUES

As technology advances, so do the avenues for library placement. Printed materials are not the only resources libraries provide their users. Many readers are now acquiring lots of their material without ever setting foot in the library. Given this truth, libraries want to make sure they are still a viable outlet for readers who otherwise might feel the library has nothing to offer them. Libraries have made partnerships with platforms such as

OverDrive, which provide access to digital works for library patrons. Such platforms also provide indie authors with a way to bring their work into libraries as well. Of course, the material must still be purchased via regular library channels, but authors are permitted to have their work evaluated for addition into the platform's catalog. As it pertains to printed work, many on-demand publishers have partnerships that get their releases into libraries. CreateSpace offers such a service provided an author uses an ISBN provided by CreateSpace as opposed to the author's own since this will list CreateSpace as the book's publisher instead of the author.

IN CLOSING

The landscape is definitely changing in terms of the library/indie publications tug of war. I find evidence of this whenever I check holdings of my independent titles. Those titles are appearing in greater numbers in libraries across the country. Readers have been the driving force behind this change in my situation. I am noticing that some libraries now seem to be taking the reins from my readers and are placing my indie releases on order shortly after they become available. While I attribute this success to the efforts of my readers, I feel that this shift is happening across the board. Independently published titles are garnering an increasing awareness and with it the respect once reserved for traditionally published works. Reviewers are recognizing the talent and diligence of indie authors while libraries are making more room on their shelves or e-book platforms for such deserving works. It is all a work in progress, and the possibilities seem extremely positive.

12 | The Romance of Self-Publishing

Elizabeth Nelson, McHenry County College

Writing a work of fiction is like putting a little of yourself on the page. It is a process that requires creativity, inspiration, and persistence. But once the words are there, where do you go next? There is an outline—a beginning, a middle, and an end to the story—but, when the writing ends, the real work begins. Many authors don't fully appreciate what it takes to get a work of fiction published. There are entire books, Web sites, and blogs devoted to helping authors understand what publishers are looking for and how to get a manuscript reviewed and accepted for publication. And to complicate matters, each publisher is looking for a different format, genre, and intended audience. But, at the same time, many authors are also familiar with the stories of now famous authors who had their first novels rejected many times over. The time required to sell a book to a publisher can be immense; and, instead of the very real prospect of facing rejection and frustration, authors now have the option to turn to self-publishing as a way to connect their book with an audience right away. Technology now allows authors to publish print books using print on demand through services like CreateSpace or to publish their own e-books that readers can download to their computer or other devices.

My own story, a romance novel set in the Regency era, began with a well-thought-out plan to follow the guidelines for a particular publisher. I wrote to the prescribed format, word count, and general tone of the story from my familiarity with the genre as a reader of romance novels. After including everything necessary in the online submission form, I hit submit and waited. And waited. I eventually learned that my story had not made it through the review process; but, in the meantime, I had explored discussion boards and blogs and found that there were many other aspiring authors in the same situation.

As an avid reader, I knew that my story was good and would have an audience if I could get it into the hands (or e-readers) of romance readers. So I started doing my research. The first decision I had to make was whether to rewrite my story and submit it to another publisher or to look into the options for self-publishing. Having just completed the writing process and happy with the completed work, I decided to keep the story mostly as it was, do some minor editing, and self-publish rather than expanding and changing the story to fit the guidelines of other publishers. After looking at the options out there, I decided to make my story into an e-book. It seemed fairly straightforward to post an electronic file online, and it allowed me to maintain control of my book while making changes as necessary. While I had written articles for library publications, I had never written a book or even a book chapter, so I knew I had a lot to learn. Using an electronic format would allow me to make changes as I went along if they proved necessary.

GETTING STARTED

At the time, there were, and still are, two main options for self-publishing fiction in an e-book format. One is Smashwords, which distributes titles through the Apple iBooks store, Barnes & Noble, and more; and the other is Amazon, which distributes titles through its Web site. While it is possible to use both Smashwords and Amazon Kindle Direct Publishing (KDP), Amazon requires exclusivity in order to take advantage of some of the features such as KDP Select and Kindle Unlimited. But whichever is chosen, the fact remains that both of these sites require the author to do most of the heavy lifting in regard to producing and promoting the e-book and provide royalties to the author only when a copy of the book sells. This requires a lot of work for the author upfront before seeing the book in final form, but it also creates the possibility for a wider range of outcomes in terms of creativity and financial benefits.

Smashwords seems to have the simpler of the two systems. Authors receive an 85% royalty of the net sales for titles sold through www.smash words.com and an 81.5% royalty of the net sales for titles sold through its affiliates ("Smashwords Support Center FAQ"). Royalty payments in excess of 80% are essentially unheard of in traditional publishing and provide a great opportunity for those who are willing to go it alone. But as was previously mentioned, the author earns those royalties by doing all the work that a publisher would usually do—from editing and formatting to setting the price and doing all the promoting and marketing.

Based on my own experiences with Amazon and the ease of using the site to make purchases, as well as the popularity of the Amazon Kindle, I decided to sell my book exclusively through Amazon KDP. Amazon offers two options for royalty payments and allows authors to select a 35% royalty or a 70% royalty. While this may seem like an easy choice, books that receive the 70% royalty must be priced between $2.99 and $9.99, which is where Amazon likes to see e-books priced. Additionally, the 70% royalty is only available for books sold in certain countries and also has the delivery costs subtracted from the price of the book before the royalty is calculated. The delivery costs are based on the size of the electronic file after it has been converted into a Kindle-friendly format ("Pricing Page"). There are additional restrictions on the pricing of the title as well, so it is simpler, if not as lucrative, to go with the 35% royalty option. Part of the process of listing a book for sale includes selecting the countries in which the author has the rights to this book. Based on that selection, titles are listed on all the Amazon sites that are appropriate, such as Amazon.com, Amazon.co.uk, Amazon.fr, and others. Pricing can be set individually for each country or can be calculated based on the U.S. price.

I decided to go with the 35% royalty option because it was more important to me to have readers purchase and read my book than to make money. I set my price at $0.99, and it has been there ever since, except for the few days when I tried raising it to see what effect the increase would have. Sales slowed down, and I readjusted the price back down to the $0.99 minimum. Pricing a title is difficult, especially when keeping the potential royalty rates in mind. For Amazon the critical price is $2.99, where a title enters into the 70% royalty rate (if selected). But for an author without much of a following it is possible to go as low as $0.99 in order to attract readers. At that level, the royalty per sale is $0.35, which isn't a lot per sale but does add up quickly as more titles are sold. While books can be sold through other Amazon sites, royalties from each site accumulate separately so it can be difficult to judge what the royalty payments might look like. Additionally, sales are conducted in the currency of the country where the sale occurs while payments are made in U.S. dollars so there are also exchange rate fluctuations to account for. This makes for a lot of moving pieces, but Amazon does provide a dashboard to monitor sales and estimated royalties as well as actual royalties paid.

CREATING A BOOK

Once the big decisions have been made, it is time to actually create the book in a Kindle-friendly format. There are companies that will provide this service, or authors have the option to do it themselves. As most books are written using a word processor, this requires a file conversion (or two) to get the file into a format that can be uploaded to Amazon KDP. In addition to doing the file conversion, the original must also be cleaned up so the final Kindle version doesn't have any extra spaces or overlapping text. There is documentation available to help authors through this process; but, for those not familiar with what needs to be done, it can take a while to get it right. In addition to formatting the text and any front matter, authors also have to create a cover. This is a new area for many authors, and the cover design is very important since it displays very prominently on Amazon.com. As with the formatting of the book, there are also companies that will design covers; or it can be done by the author. I designed my own cover by using a photo that I have the rights to and then edited it to add text with the title and author. The cover, which needs to be saved as an image file, gets combined with the rest of the book upon upload.

In writing about it now, this process seems very straightforward; but, in my first attempt, it took quite a bit of trial and error to get it right. What looks like a perfectly formatted book on a computer screen looks completely different when viewed through the previewer. In fact, even after getting through the entire process and having the book go live, I had to fix the formatting again after I tested the download and found that there were still errors. Once the book has been proofread, formatted, converted, a cover created, and the files uploaded, it is time to create the book details. All of this information is pretty standard: title, author, series, edition, a description of the book, and an ISBN if the author has obtained one. ISBN numbers are standard in the bookselling and library worlds but less important on Amazon since Amazon has created its own system. Each product on Amazon is given an ASIN (Amazon Standard Identification Number), which operates as a unique identifier within that marketplace. This is the number that appears in the description of the item on Amazon's Web site. I have opted not to obtain an ISBN since my book is self-contained within Amazon's site. However, if I decided to forgo exclusivity with Amazon and publish through Smashwords as well, I would obtain an ISBN first.

GOING IT ALONE

When deciding to self-publish, the author must wear a variety of hats. Instead of turning over the manuscript and waiting to learn about the marketing plan, a self-published author has to go through the entire process. Some of the tasks are similar to writing, like proofreading and making edits. Authors tend to bounce story ideas off friends and family anyway, so finding someone to help proofread is not a stretch. Other readers are very good at pointing out problems with the storyline or grammatical errors. But once that part is complete, you really enter into the unknown. There is formatting and converting the file, creating bibliographic information, and doing your own marketing. Prices and promotions can be tweaked depending on sales. Taking care of your book can take as much or as little time as you have. Some authors constantly blog about and promote their books while others post the title and let it do its own magic. But there are a few basic steps that can make a difference.

Amazon is really its own ecosystem. In addition to listing titles, Amazon also has author pages. Author pages list an author's books, have discussion boards, and allow authors to post a picture and biography. This provides a contact point for readers and allows authors to share information about upcoming books and more. In addition, readers can review books on Amazon. Five-star reviews are gold as they tend to attract even more readers.

In addition to using what is provided by Amazon, getting out into the wider Web is important. My book is also listed on Goodreads and has received reviews there as well. When my book first went live on Amazon, I reached out to several bloggers who reviewed romance books to see if I could get my e-book reviewed. Creating buzz leads to more readers; but it is difficult to get a self-published book, particularly a self-published e-book, into the hands of reviewers. And as far as romance bloggers are concerned, they will never run out of books to review so adding one more to the pile isn't the best option. But even without wider-reaching reviews, readers have found my book through Amazon and Goodreads and allowed me to focus my efforts elsewhere. Goodreads also has author pages that allow authors to connect with readers, and the size of that community makes it worthwhile to spend the time to create a profile.

BECOMING A PUBLISHED AUTHOR

Once a book is loaded, there is a delay in finding the book on Amazon.com. There is a review of the material to make sure it isn't copyrighted or illegal, though Amazon doesn't provide any proofreading of the final book. As soon as my book was officially live and I could search for myself on Amazon, I was really a published author. The months of work leading up to that moment were all worth it. With the sheer number of books published each year, it is amazing that there are enough readers to keep up with all of them. But in some sense, "if you build it, they will come." Especially with romance readers, there is a home for every new book. I started selling my book right away and haven't looked back.

In the time since my book was first published in 2011 I have taken advantage of some of the programs that Amazon offers. As long as they retain exclusivity with Amazon, authors can enroll their books in KDP Select. This essentially unlocks all the extra features. Titles in KDP Select become part of Kindle Unlimited and Kindle Owners' Lending Library (KOLL). Kindle Unlimited is the program in which, for a subscription fee, readers can read as many books as they want while KOLL is a program that lets Kindle Owners who also subscribe to Amazon Prime read one free book a month. The benefit to authors is that instead of getting the royalty rate for titles that are purchased, authors get a share of the KDP Select Global Fund. This fund is awarded monthly to authors who have had books borrowed through KOLL or have had a certain percentage of the book read through Kindle Unlimited ("Why Enroll in KDP Select?"). This is an advantage to authors who receive royalties at the 35% rate or who have titles that are priced fairly low. Depending on the number of books borrowed or read during the month, an author's share of the KDP Select Global Fund can be substantial. On the other hand, authors who have priced their titles higher and/or are receiving royalties at the 70% rate could actually get less from the KDP Select Global Fund than they would get if the book had been purchased.

Additionally, enrollment in KDP Select also means that authors can use promotions like Kindle Countdown Deals or Free Book Promotion to generate more interest in the title. Taking advantage of these promotions does require exclusivity with Amazon and only reaches those readers who already use Amazon, but it does provide a quick way to promote a book without investing a lot of time or money. The only downside is that there are pricing restrictions on books that can be promoted via Kindle Countdown Deals though the Free Book Promotion can be used on books at any price.

WAS IT A SUCCESS?

Overall, I have had a very positive experience with e-books, self-publishing, and Amazon KDP. While there have been some bumps in the road, they were not insurmountable. At several points during the process, I have had the opportunity to purchase services for editing the book, designing a cover, marketing the book, and more. I have chosen to go with a very bare-bones approach since this is my first effort. I think that, if I were to do it again, I would take advantage of some of these services. I had no idea what was going to happen. I didn't know if I would be wasting my money and no one would buy the book or if I even needed to worry about those things. But having gone through the process, I now know the importance of the design of a book cover. It is worth the investment to have a professional design the book cover. Even in the world of e-books, the cover of the book is the most important factor in engaging readers. The cover has to make an impression on readers that are scanning through the thumbnail images looking for their next book. On the other hand, formatting the book is time consuming but doesn't really require any special expertise. As long as the book is primarily text and follows the formatting guidelines, there isn't much of a reason to pay someone else to do this work, though a good proofreader is a must.

But above all, self-published authors need to market and promote their books. As with any other endeavor, it is important to have a Web presence. Author pages on Amazon and Goodreads are a good first step, but it is important to get in front of readers and keep them engaged. This might mean blogging or connecting with other bloggers. It also means responding to readers and remaining active. This is an area where I have not done a great job and could use the help of someone who knows about marketing e-books. Having connections to authors or bloggers who can share links or provide reviews goes a long way in spreading the word about a book.

However, part of my problem stems from the fact that I don't write fiction under my real name. Having a separate pen name means twice as much work in taking advantage of social media and maintaining a Web presence. Writing while having another career means that the time for professional activities has to come from somewhere, and it often comes out of the time I would have spent writing and marketing. As a librarian I appreciate the concept of separate bibliographic identities, but if I had chosen to write under my name, then I could have better utilized my existing network to promote my e-book.

From a financial standpoint, I have been pleased with the results I've seen. I went into this not really having any expectations; but I have had sales since I first published my e-book more than three years ago, and I continue to receive royalty checks each month. My sales come mostly from Amazon.com and Amazon.co.uk though my book is listed on all of the Amazon marketplaces. Royalties have been in the hundreds of dollars with the number of readers nearing the thousands. Not enough to quit my day job and write full-time, but enough to serve as a proof of concept. I have another Regency romance that I've been working on; and, once it is finished, I plan to add it to my bookshelf on Amazon KDP. Having two titles listed will allow me to take better advantage of the promotions since offering free books or discounts can lead readers to pay full price for other titles.

I don't think that my experience using Amazon KDP is unusual. There are a lot of authors self-publishing their books in an electronic format, and Amazon has created a community and ecosystem that make it "easy" to be successful. While not every part of the process is easy, especially the formatting and uploading of the book, the entire process is fairly seamless. There are instructions to follow and a supportive community if the documentation doesn't fully solve the problem. Amazon has also become the preferred destination for online shoppers, especially for Kindle owners looking for a new book to download, so that small successes lead to more sales and more sales lead to increased visibility on Amazon. Amazon KDP really puts the tools in front of the author. The book listings and the author pages are standardized and professional. There is no difference between the author page of a self-published author and the page of a best-selling author.

E-books are a great option for those looking to self-publish because there are no up-front costs, except the ones that you choose to incur. There is no printing and no storage because there is no inventory. For an author that is just getting started or writing for a hobby, Amazon provides a low-cost, low–time commitment way to get a book published. And while self-published authors don't get the support that comes from a traditional publisher, they have the opportunity to make something that is entirely their own with no strings attached.

REFERENCES

Pricing page. *Kindle direct publishing*. Amazon. Retrieved from https://kdp.amazon.com/help?topicId=A29FL26OKE7R7B

Smashwords Support Center FAQ. Smashwords. Retrieved from http://www.smashwords.com/about/supportfaq

Why enroll in KDP Select? *Kindle direct publishing*. Amazon. Retrieved from https://kdp.amazon.com/select

13 | Alacrity House Publishing

Frankie L. Colton, Alacrity House Publishing

Alacrity House Publishing was founded in answer to a desire to showcase the tremendous talent of people living in the San Luis Valley in Colorado. In the spring of 2010, my husband and I retired and moved to a small (population 750) town in the San Luis Valley. I grew up in Sanford, Colorado, couldn't wait to leave, was reluctant to think of returning to the small-town atmosphere, but decided to take a chance on it anyway. Our daughter, Linda, and her three children joined the adventure and moved to Sanford from Eugene, Oregon.

Linda and I wanted to join a writing group. We inquired at libraries, Adams State University, and other places we hoped might know about such a group, but found nothing. We decided to start our own. We hung up flyers in libraries, in the post office window, and at grocery stores in each of the small towns nearby. Our first meeting was held around the dining room table at our home. Five or six people attended our twice monthly meetings, although one time nobody came. Meetings featured presentations devoted to improving writing skills and preparing for publication. We shared our writing and discussed ways to improve it.

So what, you ask, does this have to do with a publishing business? As the months passed, I was impressed with the talent of members of the slowly growing group of writers. On the first of December 2011, during our meeting, I said: "One of these days we need to publish a collection of our writing. And today is the day to start. Send me a couple of your favorite pieces of writing by January 15, 2012, and we'll see about getting it published."

BEGINNINGS

That was the beginning of Alacrity House Publishing. As Terry, Linda, and I discussed the project, we considered the publishing options available to us. Realizing that the anthology we were planning to publish was of a limited, regional appeal, we began to research the possibilities. Linda had experience working with Lulu and Memory Press in her personal history business. We talked to the one local printer, who would print our book from the electronic file we would furnish, but who offered no editorial or design services. We investigated many online publishing companies for both traditional publishing and self-publishing. We considered what services we needed and what the cost would be.

By December 21, 2011, we had decided to form our own publishing company and completed the paperwork to get started as Alacrity House Publishing. The name Alacrity House Publishing was chosen because alacrity means cheerful readiness, promptness, liveliness—qualities we desired for our company. We were ready to begin our business as publishers. We would publish the anthology for our writing group, books written by local authors, as well as our own books.

Alacrity's mission is to offer superior service and quality products to southern Colorado authors and artists seeking publication. The San Luis Valley, average elevation 7,600 feet, is a large alpine valley in southern Colorado and northern New Mexico. In this rural area, potatoes, alfalfa, and barley are important crops. The Valley is home to two of the poorest counties in Colorado but is rich in heritage and cultural traditions from the original Ute Indian inhabitants; to settlers from Mexico; to Mormons, miners, and others who came here to live. Talent abounds in the San Luis Valley, but low incomes and lack of information keep many from trying to publish their work. Preserving the heritage of the Valley and helping writers and artists to publish their work is a primary focus for Alacrity House Publishing.

We were in need of something of a crash course in publishing since I had set the deadline for publication of our first book ridiculously soon. In order to learn more about the publishing business, we joined the Colorado Independent Publishers Association (CIPA), the Independent Book Publishers Association (IBPA), and the Association of Publishers for Special Sales (APSS). Being book people and researchers by nature and experience, we invested in a basic collection of books for reference and information. Some of these are listed in the References section of this chapter.

PUBLISHING

With the legalities and organization completed, it was time to prepare our first book for publication. For the first volume of *The Circle Book: A Conejos County Anthology 2012,* we used everything that was submitted and edited rather freely (with the permission of the writers). Submissions of both written and art entries were accepted and organized into a preliminary order by Frankie Colton. Book design and layout were done by Linda Anderson Smith, using Microsoft Word. Research about printers, both local and online, was done by Terry Colton. Quotes for the print job were compared, along with formatting requirements and time required to submit the electronic files and receive the books. Editing and proofreading were done by everyone—Frankie, Linda, and Terry. We learned a lot about the possibility for errors during that process. We read, read, and reread the draft, and still found little errors—typos, widows and orphans, misalignment of pages. We went through the draft time after time to make sure the page numbers were correct, that the facing pages were correct, that the fonts were correct. When the manuscript was ready, Terry Colton converted the files to a PDF for submission to the printer, and the proofreading began again to make sure nothing had fallen out of place during the PDF conversion. One of the biggest challenges was making the table of contents useful and look right. Titles and page numbers were listed. When we were finished, we realized that people wanted to look for the names of the writers and artists rather than looking for the title of the piece. The book was already printed, so we created a bookmark to place in each book that listed the author or artist with page numbers.

We published two books during that first rush from December 2011 to February 2012. We did everything from selection of material, to typing some submissions that were submitted in handwritten rather than electronic form, to book layout, to cover design, and to preparation of the files for submission to an online printer. Book release parties were planned and advertised in the local newspapers with flyers placed in libraries, post office windows (these are small communities, remember), and grocery store bulletin boards. Two books were released in March 2012: *The Circle Book: A Conejos County Anthology 2012* and *Pickin' and Pannin': Poems of Creede and Thereabouts.*

Preparing to print a quality book was not the hardest part for Alacrity House Publishing. We already had some of the necessary skills and learned others. As a former librarian, Frankie had experience with cataloging and bibliographic information as well as with acquisitions in a public school library setting. Terry had technical experience helpful in preparing e-books for varying platforms. Linda had worked with book layout and cover design. All were proficient at editing and proofreading.

Marketing processes, including getting books reviewed and securing testimonials to inform and attract those purchasing books for libraries and for personal reading, were new territory for us. We need to develop this area of expertise. In conversations with Colorado Independent Publisher Association members and self-published authors, we found that understanding what constitutes a reputable review that will carry weight with those purchasing books for libraries, schools, and personal use appears to be a source of concern, as well as how to go about getting such a review. Anyone planning to publish would be wise to learn about the process and implement it as part of the marketing plan.

Alacrity House Publishing uses a traditional publishing format with Alacrity House offering a contract to authors. Alacrity House pays all expenses. Authors receive royalties after initial publishing expenses are recovered. Alacrity House also offers consulting services to authors who wish to self-publish but who need help with specific aspects of preparing their books for publication. Editing, book layout, cover design, and proofreading are available at a reasonable hourly rate as well as a preliminary consultation about the steps involved in preparing a book for publication.

During the preliminary consultation, authors who inquire about our publishing services are introduced to the Alacrity House philosophy and the contract and royalty arrangements. We answer questions about traditional vs. self-publishing and encourage authors to choose a reputable publisher that they can afford and that will provide the services they need as well as helping them determine what services they actually will need.

After this initial consultation, two authors chose to have their books published by Alacrity House Publishing; and two authors chose to use self-publishing companies and to purchase packages of services varying from basic printing to packages that include marketing materials and other services. Those who have utilized other companies have not purchased the editing services and have chosen to do their own editing or to use friends and family to help with editing and proofreading. Two authors are waiting to make a decision about publishing.

One author who contacted Alacrity House Publishing chose to self-publish using Author House. She purchased a package that included marketing materials such as posters, bookmarks, postcards, and listings on Amazon and Barnes & Noble. Her cover was designed by Author House, using some of her photos and ideas. She did not purchase editing services but used friends and family to do editing and proofreading. She is now working on her second book.

Phil Ray Jack, who consulted with Alacrity House Publishing about things to look for in a publisher, has written a short summary of his experience in self-publishing with Abbott Press that is included at the end of this chapter. He is releasing his second book soon.

BOOKS

Alacrity House Publishing has published six books, listed below, since 2012.

The Circle Book: A Conejos County Anthology 2012. Compiled by the Conejos Writers Circle. This compilation includes the work of writers and artists who live, work, and find inspiration in Conejos County. Included are poetry, essays, short stories, photos, and original art work. This book was awarded Second Place for Anthology in the Colorado Independent Publishers Association EVVY Award competition.

The Circle Book: A Conejos County Anthology 2013. Compiled by the Conejos Writers Circle. In addition to poetry, essays, short stories, photos, and sayings submitted by adults, writing and artwork from students in the local schools are included.

The Circle Book: A Conejos County Anthology 2014. Compiled by the Conejos Writers Circle. In addition to poetry, essays, short stories, photos, and sayings submitted by adults, writing and artwork from students in the local schools are included. This book is a finalist in the Anthology division of the Colorado Book Awards.

The Circle Book: A Conejos County Anthology 2015. Compiled by the Conejos Writers Circle. In addition to poetry, essays, short stories, photos, and sayings submitted by adults, writing and artwork from students in the local schools are included.

Cisneros, Lucy and Chris. *The Tale of Honest Henrietta: La Historia de Enriqueta la Honesta.* A tale about friendship and honesty, this children's bilingual storybook about a chicken was written by Lucy and illustrated by Chris. It includes a short section of chicken facts and is available with a companion coloring book and small stuffed chicken toys.

Miller, Mary June. *Pickin' and Pannin': Poems of Creede and Thereabouts.* This delightful, down-to-earth peek at the West of yesteryear uses historical tidbits and tales about Creede and neighboring places to bring back characters like Nicholas Creede, Jesse James, Bob Ford, Poker Alice, and Soapy Smith. Both soft- and hardcover versions were produced.

Steppingstones of Our Lives, by Frankie Colton, will be published in 2015.

Dr. Terry Colton is preparing to publish a series of how-to books. Linda Anderson Smith's contemporary fiction novel will be published in late 2015.

LIBRARIES AND ALACRITY

We love libraries. We use libraries. We want our books to be in libraries. In an effort to make our books useful for libraries, we have focused first on quality—quality content, presentation, and binding.

Quality content is of utmost importance. People want to borrow library books that will educate them and entertain them. Writing that is well organized and grammatically correct is essential as is documentation of reliable, up-to-date sources for nonfiction. Other aspects of quality writing such as illustration and photography are considered. During the selection process for books we publish and for the contents of the anthology we publish yearly, we look for ideas that reflect the heritage of the San Luis Valley and that have a degree of universal appeal as well. As we branch out and publish books intended for a broader audience, we will continue to look for authentic, reliable, well-documented content in nonfiction and for fiction that is suitable for a larger target audience.

Presentation is key in getting readers to look beyond the cover. Good cover design, including the spine, will catch a librarian's eye in the catalog or online and a reader's eye on the library or bookstore shelf. Once the book is opened, the interior should be pleasing to the eye, easy to use, and give authentic, reliable content.

Books in public, school, academic, or specialized libraries are subjected to frequent (we hope) and sometimes hard use. Because our books thus far have been short runs of rather specialized interest, we have not provided a library binding option. Rather, we sought good-quality bindings in both softcover and hardcover books. Perfect-bound softcover books with covers that do not curl or develop loose pages were our goal as we selected a printer. Hardcover books that are sturdy and have a dust cover are our choice.

Once a quality book suitable for library use has been produced, the next step is to get the book into the appropriate libraries. Because our first books are of regional appeal, Alacrity House Publishing has worked with libraries only in the San Luis Valley. Librarians at public libraries have purchased books. We donated a copy of each book to school libraries in Conejos County where students from the schools have contributed writing or artwork. Books were also donated to the Adams State University Library. We plan in the future to utilize IBPA's library listings and other methods of advertising books to libraries.

Alacrity House Publishing has been invited to participate in author events at the Alamosa Public Library, the Conejos County Library, and the Adams State University library. These events have provided good opportunities for publicity in the local newspapers as well as for word-of-mouth communication with readers.

PRINTERS AND SERVICE PROVIDERS

After considering the local printer, printers in China and Korea, and many online printers, we chose to use DiggyPod (www.diggypod.com) to print and bind our first books. Our books featured both black-and-white and color pages. We needed only 200 copies to start with, due to the regional nature of the books. DiggyPod's prices for printing were competitive. The service was good. They were helpful and on time. Both electronic and print proofs were available. Corrections were costly but possible. There was a person, not an answering machine, on the end of the line any time we had questions. Our experience with DiggyPod was positive, and we have continued to use them for printing softcover books.

Lulu (www.lulu.com) was selected as the printer for the hardcover edition of *Pickin' and Pannin'*. The books are good quality, and the price was reasonable. Linda Anderson Smith was familiar with their work from having used Lulu in printing memoirs for clients in her personal history business.

Alacrity House Publishing (www.alacrityhousepublishing.com) did all the editing, book layout, cover design, bar codes and ISBNs, proofreading and e-book creation. We investigated the possibility of consulting editors and book designers who were members of CIPA and whose businesses provided those services; but, with their prices of $125 per hour, we chose to do our own work. Alacrity House Publishing now offers editing plus book layout and cover design services at an affordable hourly rate.

CHALLENGES

We learned a lot from that first, intense push to get two books ready on schedule. Submissions for *The Circle Book* now go through a selection process rather than our using everything submitted. Since that time, we have streamlined the book production process by creating a flowchart for the procedures and responsibilities. We now use Adobe's InDesign to create the layout for book interiors and covers.

Marketing remains a challenge for Alacrity House Publishing. We recognize the need to make our books available in markets beyond the local bookstores, arts and crafts events, library book signings, and limited online avenues for sales. We need to make greater use of libraries and book signings to promote our books. We need to go beyond newspaper and word of mouth and to include reviews and testimonials to help promote our books. IBPA can be a help in getting library listings and book show opportunities. We are preparing media kits that include bookmarks, postcards, and posters to help with marketing.

PLANS FOR THE FUTURE

As we expand from our initial publication of the *Anthology* for the Conejos Writers Circle, we are publishing children's books, poetry, and self-help/how-to books, including more universal topics along with our regional focus. E-books and online marketing are areas we plan to expand and improve. We will be investigating the use of IBPA library lists and book shows.

ORGANIZATIONS

The following are lists of organizations that have been helpful to us:
Association of Publishers for Special Sales (APSS) (http://www.spanpro .org/). APSS is a nonprofit trade association of authors and independent publishers with the mission of building successful writing and publishing businesses. APSS provides educational webinars, along with other services.

Colorado Independent Publishers Association (CIPA) (http://www.cipa catalog.com). CIPA's mission is to encourage cooperative efforts and the free exchange of information, experience, and expertise to help members achieve and prosper while also assisting the writing and marketing of their books through cooperative ventures, education, and networking. Monthly meetings feature guest presenters on topics such as marketing and copyright. CIPA also sponsors the EVVY awards each year for books published by independent publishers.

Independent Book Publishers Association (IBPA) (http://www.ibpa online .org/). IBPA's mission is to lead and serve the independent publishing community by providing advocacy, education, and tools for success. IBPA's magazine, *Independent*, has articles about all aspects of publishing including book layout, editing, and marketing to libraries, chain stores, and online. The advertising serves as a resource for finding publishing services as well as for information about what other publishers are doing and charging. IBPA sponsors a yearly Publishing University. IBPA membership and resources are a valuable tool.

REFERENCE SOURCES

The following are some reference sources that have been helpful. There are many more on my shelf. This list is a beginning that gives some of the most useful.

Chicago Manual of Style (16th ed.). (2010). Chicago: The University of Chicago Press. This is an essential tool for answering technical questions about punctuation, grammar, format, and so on.

Levine, M. (2011). *The Fine Print of Self-Publishing* (4th ed.). Minneapolis, MN: Bascom Hill Publishing Group. From Dan Poynter, *Self-Publishing Manual*, "If you're considering paying a company to publish your book, don't do anything until you read *The Fine Print* and consider the alternatives. It will save you a lot of time, money, and heartache." Information about costs, contracts, the process of self-publishing, and a useful evaluation of a number of self-publishing companies.

Merriam Webster's Collegiate Dictionary (11th ed.). (2011). Springfield, MA: Merriam Webster. Don't ignore the necessity of having a good dictionary close at hand.

Miller, J. L., & Miller, C. D. (2013). *Copyright Clearance for Creatives: A Guide for Independent Publishers and Their Support Providers.*

Denver, CO: Integrated Writer Services. This book gives solid, in-depth information about copyright.

Poynter, D. (2010). *Self-Publishing Manual: How to Write, Print and Sell Your Own Book* (16th ed.). Santa Barbara, CA: Para Publishing. Dan Poynter has produced several helpful books about self-publishing, writing nonfiction, and other topics.

Ross, M., & Collier, S. (2010). *The Complete Guide to Self Publishing* (5th ed.). Cincinnati, OH: Writers Digest Books. Discusses writing, publishing, promoting, and selling your self-published book.

CONCLUDING THOUGHTS

Since our first venture into the world of publishing, prompted by our desire to help preserve the rich cultural heritage of the unique San Luis Valley where we live, we at Alacrity House Publishing have learned many valuable lessons. We know our strengths and weaknesses and have a goal of improving as we produce and promote quality books.

APPENDIX

"Self-Publishing and Self-Promoting" by Phil Ray Jack, self-published author:

When I gave in to that inner voice that demanded I express myself through the written word, I didn't realize I had a choice, but since I've become a "real author," I often ask myself why I do it. Sometimes I ask other writers the same question. One of the most powerful responses I received was, "I write so that I don't feel alone."

I think any discussion about the benefits and challenges of self-publishing should begin right there.

Most of us are introverts. We simply enjoy being alone, and we are at our best when we are in solitude. It's not that we can't handle social gatherings, but we tend to want to sit in the back row and observe rather than taking a place on the stage. The thought of being the center of attention is terrifying for many of us. For others, it's simply exhausting. We may endure it, but we are anxious to return to the peace of our work areas and lose ourselves in the world of words.

So, once we finish capturing that little piece of our souls in words, we would like to turn them over to someone who will treasure them as much as we do and present them to the world in all their glory and majesty.

Unfortunately, the traditional publishers I approached with my first book were not nearly as thrilled with my work as I was. It's hard to not take rejection personally—in fact, I still haven't figured out how to do so. It was discouraging, and I would have given up if I knew how to.

Eventually I realized that I was putting too much control of my happiness in the hands of faceless strangers, and I began looking into self-publishing. I was shopping around in almost complete ignorance, but fortunately I found a publisher that offered support services and enlisted their help. The lessons I've learned have been worth every penny.

I discovered that no one—not even my publisher—will ever have the same love for my work or believe in it nearly as much as I do. There's nothing wrong with that. Our roles are simply different. And even though I self-published, I finally realized I was still putting my dream in the hands of faceless strangers as long as I waited for them to market my work.

But I also discovered I had a lot to learn about publishing and marketing, and while some of the services offered didn't seem to accomplish much, I learned from the experience. Other services were extremely valuable. Quite frankly, not having to deal with the process of getting an ISBN number for my book made the whole experience worthwhile.

14 | Self-Publishing: A Bibliographic Essay

Joseph D. Grobelny, Front Range Community College

As institutions, libraries have relied on publishers to act as bellwethers for the building of collections; and, as a result, publishers and their distributors have been tightly integrated into our workflows in a highly efficient system of physical and intellectual bibliographic control. This has left the relationship between authors who self-publish and libraries somewhat fraught with difficulty. With the rise of e-books, significant disruptions to the publishing industry have opened up the field for authors to self-publish titles at such rates that libraries can no longer ignore them. While the current trend of self-publishing is not entirely driven by e-books, research presented in 2011 by Kelly Gallagher, vice president of publisher services for Bowker, suggests that while e-books make less money, they move the most individual units.[1] Gallagher's research also provides insights as to the content of the self-publishing market with the unsurprising result that, while fiction also moves more units, it makes less money than nonfiction. In short, while self-publishing has always been a problem for libraries and publishers, the ease of self-publishing e-books has made it impossible to ignore the vast increase in the number of titles. More recent surveys of U.S. ISBN data in 2013 by the publisher Bowker peg the number of self-published titles at 391,000, a 59% increase from 2011;[2] and other selective surveys of Amazon Bestseller lists indicate that the Big Five publishers make it only 16% of the time.[3] In the mass market in particular, the real story of self-publishing and libraries is a question of volume. This is a selective essay designed to introduce this vast topic. While much has been contributed to the literature, the intention in this chapter is to provide the general contours of self-publishing and libraries over the last 10 years.

To get a better sense of the self-publishing market, a good place to start is Jana Bradley et al.'s *Non-Traditional Book Publishing*,[4] which defines and roughly measures a number of nontraditional publishing avenues from self-published e-books to publisher-supported "nontraditional" publishing. To support the idea that self-publishing is currently driven by e-books, they found that the sales of self-published print books averaged in the hundreds per year (with a handful of exceptional titles) and that only 27% of the sample titles were held by libraries. Of note, in the self-published e-book section, libraries are not mentioned as these titles tend to be sold through a platform directly to the consumer. The idea that libraries are being bypassed in the self-published e-book market is supported by another article by the same group of authors using similar data:[5] in a 348-title sample from 2008, they found only 102 that were held by at least one OCLC member library though 98% of the sample was still available for purchase in 2010. At the very least, it is clear that libraries are not large buyers of self-published e-books. The impression given by Bradley and her coauthors is that, since self-published books are often overlooked by the library/publisher dyad, it will take new kinds of discovery tools to make them accessible. This conclusion may miss the crucial point: discovery, along with production, is largely happening elsewhere.

PUBLISHERS

If libraries have generally overlooked the self-publishing trend, the book industry as a whole has been incredibly responsive. Anecdotal evidence of traditional publishers being bypassed by authors, as in the case of best-selling thriller author Blake Crouch,[6] understates the fact that he started out publishing four books with St. Martin's Press before becoming a DIY (do-it-yourself) published author. E-books were the primary driver of his move away from traditional publishers. The anecdotes continue to support the idea that having some kind of institutional support is desirable. A number of children's authors, after beginning in self-publishing, signed deals with major publishing groups.[7] Such support comes not only from traditional publishers, but also from their biggest competitor, Amazon. The Amazon Kindle Direct Program gets several mentions in *Publishers Weekly*'s

"Select" section, which focuses on self-publishing and also shares success stories for self-published authors[8] and for such groups as Lulu.com and others. To compete in the new self-publishing marketplace, members of the Big Five publishers have been acquiring smaller self-publishing groups that expand the traditional publishers' technological reach, as is the case of the Penguin Group's acquisition of Author Solutions.[9]

The proliferation of self-published titles has largely been a marketing-driven move to capture the "long tail" that e-books provide. Bradley and others have lamented that this expanding volume of works is not easily searched by librarians' discovery tools, especially since self-published books provide a wealth of information by nonacademic experts.[10] Traditional gatekeeping roles could fall by the wayside due to market forces. Ann Haugland, University of Iowa, in a great essay on traditional royalty publishers, print-on-demand subsidy publishers, and wholly self-published authors, applies the lens of cultural production (Howard Becker's *Art Worlds* and Raymond William's *Sociology of Culture*) to find that new gatekeepers such as Mystery Writers of America have begun to take over the function traditionally left to publishers of validating these amateur forms of cultural production.[11]

PUBLIC LIBRARIES

In the meantime, public libraries have led the way in dealing with self-publishing. Given that fiction tends to drive self-publishing and e-books, Juris Dilevko and Keren Dali's 2006 paper on self-publishing and libraries contains few surprises but many illuminating facts. It begins with a comprehensive literature review of self-publishing in the 20th century and focuses on the growth of three self-publishing houses: AuthorHouse, iUniverse, and Xlibris, all print-on-demand services that got their start in the 1990s. Their literature review of libraries and their relationship with such services reveals a consistently skeptical stance toward their products.[12] More importantly, it provides the earliest data on library holdings. Among the types of libraries, public libraries were twice as likely to hold self-published titles, largely in fiction, U.S. history, and the social sciences, especially for titles from the above-mentioned services.

Like much of the discussion around self-publishing, economics are of primary concern for publishers and public libraries alike. In a column for *The Digital Shift*, Jamie LaRue, director of Douglas County Public Libraries

(Colorado), examines the economic strains put upon public libraries by the Big Five publishers (*All Hat, No Cattle*).[13] His response was making e-book deals with 12 groups of publishers (800+ companies).[14] In addition to this model of finding smaller publisher partners who are willing to provide e-books directly to libraries, public libraries have been leaders in implementing print-on-demand (POD) publishing services through the availability of Espresso Book Machines.[15] This step ties public libraries to the spirit of maker culture where locally produced goods are highly valued. This trend is echoed in the sentiments of the 3-D printer crowd in academic libraries and is tied to the move from traditional academic libraries to the Information Commons in the early and mid-2000s. Nonetheless, looking at the list of locations that provide POD services, public libraries are in the minority compared to independent booksellers and university bookstores. Outside a higher rate of collecting and occasional forays into POD, the story of self-publishing and public libraries is largely unresearched, albeit widely discussed.

ACADEMIC LIBRARIES

If one piece of writing should be considered representative of the directions that academic libraries have taken and will continue to take in regard to self-publishing, it is Carpenter et al.'s *Envisioning the Library's Role in Scholarly Communication in the Year 2025*.[16] In a survey of selected library directors, this study found that a number of them saw an important role for the academic library as publisher and facilitator of scholarly publishing. A majority of them saw the economics of scholarly publishing as a driving factor. Such concerns were, however, less important than defining new subject-specialized and faculty roles for librarians and aligning libraries more closely with the pedagogical interests of MLIS programs. This viewpoint might reflect either the surrender of libraries to the goal of increasing market forces in collection development or the arrival of a much more service-oriented institution in both teaching and knowledge creation services and facilities.

In the survey article *Research Library Publishing Services: New Options for University Publishing*,[17] a high number (70–80%) of libraries published journals, proceedings, and monographs. They also saw great demand for hosting services and much demand for publishing consultation services. In light of limited resources, academic library publishing tends to be simple, open access, and volunteer-run to avoid the higher costs of providing subscription services. The authors noted: "[T]here appears to be no dominant sequence of service evolution, but publishing services are co-managed and often integrated with a range of new services such as digitization initiatives, digital humanities initiatives, digital repository deployment, development of learning objects, digital preservation activities." Similar and more recent research can also be found in Walter's *The Future Role of Publishing Services in University Libraries*.[18] Because of the "pay for it twice" model that academic libraries operate under, issues of copyright in the publication of journal articles have had interesting effects that influence the ways that academic authors self-publish.

There is, however, a counterpoint to this optimism. In their article *Digital Repositories Ten Years On*, Nichols et al. found that library directors considered the resources spent on library article repositories "very modest indeed" and that they are not thought to "herald a major reform of the scholarly communication and publishing system."[19] That is not exactly a vote of confidence in a major part of libraries' contribution to self-publishing, but it does recognize the limited role that libraries play in the practice. There is very little research on the acquisition of self-published materials by academic libraries. As opposed to public libraries, academic ones are positioning themselves to be publishers themselves.

COPYRIGHT AND SELF-ARCHIVING

Kristin Antelman's *Self-Archiving Practice and the Influence of Publisher Policies in the Social Sciences*[20] found that, in a group of select social science journals, more self-archiving happened for articles in journals that prohibited it than those that did not. Clearly, some academic authors feel the need to rely on their home institution's services rather than a publisher's. Such outright disobedience (willful or not) is interesting in light of the increasing opportunities for authors to legally participate in self-archiving. The clearest discussion of why this occurs is found in *Communication Regimes in Competition: The Current Transition in Scholarly Communication Seen through the Lens of the Sociology of Technology*,[21] which found in 2001 that 68–83% of preprints in arXiv were later accepted by traditional journals. The authors contend that self-archiving is primarily used for distribution, and traditional venues are used by authors for credit-allocating and quality control. A later study by Denise Covey at Carnegie

Mellon University[22] examined the publications listed by faculty on their Web sites combined with faculty interviews to determine faculty views on self-archiving. Covey notes that faculty tended to favor self-archiving recent works. She also discovered disconnects between the breadth of adoption by faculty in various disciplinary departments and the depth (number of works archived) by individual faculty members with only 11% of the faculty doing so habitually. She also found that only a minority of publisher policies forbid self-archiving, both pre- and postprint. In addition, many faculty either were unaware of the publisher's policy or disregarded it in self-archiving.

When it comes to self-archiving, two clear points emerge: first, although it runs in concert with traditional publishing avenues, the total savings to higher education could be substantial, depending on which system of open-access publishing and archiving is used, even if there would be a loss in net benefits in the short term;[23] and, second, open-access articles of any kind have significantly higher impact rates.[24]

Nichols et al. ran a similar survey project on digital repositories across a wider variety of institutions and focused on the impact that self-archiving has had on the behavior of scholars. The survey confirmed a handful of previous studies that emphasized the importance of digital repositories for the physical sciences over other disciplines but more notably that they also placed a copy of all or most of their outputs on their personal or departmental Web pages.[25] The authors wonder if this is a matter of covering formal and informal channels of distribution, which may bypass digital repositories or traditional journals, but do not consider that faculty could easily be linking to repository or other copies, further complicating the question. And while 87.3% of respondents to the survey claimed to use digital repositories to find information, they also are concerned with the difficulty of their use and the varying quality of the material. All of this supports the idea that archived journal articles may have higher impact rates.

CONCLUSION

A lot of the discussion and research on self-publishing and libraries focus on e-books and how they will disrupt "business as usual" for large, slow-moving institutions. Models focused around "disruption" are useful as catalysts for change but in practice rarely focus on long-term goals. While many readers who look at the literature on the relationship between self-publishing and libraries might conclude that libraries will soon be left behind the market, it is worth taking the longer view that libraries will most likely successfully adapt to the changed publishing environment. Given the difficult task of responding to economic pressures while still maintaining the ability to meet our communities' needs with quality and lasting access, incremental experimentation and slow consensus building are not only desirable, but preferable. This volume will be a step toward an increased understanding of the advantages and pitfalls of self-publishing. Public libraries are starting to deal with this issue because of pressure from patrons who want to read self-published materials. Academic libraries are far behind.

NOTES

1. Milliot, J. (2012). Taking the measure of self-publishing. *Publishers Weekly*, *259*(28), 1–2.
2. Dempsey, B. (2013, October 9). Self-publishing movement continues strong growth in U.S., says Bowker. Retrieved April 29, 2015, from http://www.bowkcr.com/news/2013/Self-Publishing-Movement-Continues-Strong-Growth-in-US-Says-Bowker.html
3. Sargent, B. (2014, July 28). Surprising self-publishing statistics. Retrieved April 29, 2015, from http://www.publishersweekly.com/pw/by-topic/authors/pw-select/article/63455-surprising-self-publishing-statistics.html
4. Bradley, J., Fulton, B., Helm, M., & Pittner, K. A. (2011). Non-traditional book publishing. *First Monday*, *16*(8), n.p.
5. Bradley, J., Fulton, B., & Helm, M. (2012). Self-published book: An empirical snapshot. *The Library Quarterly*, *82*(2), 107–140.
6. Schiller, K. (2011). Do-it-yourselfers. *Econtent*, *34*(5), 8–12.
7. Lodge, S. (2011). Self-published children's books thrive in the mainstream. *Publishers Weekly*, *258*(13), 6–8.
8. Palmer, A. (2012). On readers' radar. *Publishers Weekly*, *259*(52), 1–3.
9. Hane, P. J. (2012). Spotlight on the self-publishing market. *Information Today*, *29*(8), 7.
10. Bradley, J., Fulton, B., and Helm, M. (2012). Self-published book: An empirical snapshot. *The Library Quarterly*, *82*(2), 107–140.
11. Haugland, A. (2006). Opening the gates: Print on-demand publishing as cultural production. *Publishing Research Quarterly*, *22*(3), 3–16.
12. Dilevko, J., & Dali, K. (2006). The self-publishing phenomenon and libraries. *Library & Information Science Research*, *28*(2), 208–234.

13. LaRue, J. (2012). All hat, no cattle. *Library Journal, 137*(13), 32–33.

14. LaRue, J. (2012). An open letter about ebooks and Douglas County Public Libraries. http://douglascountylibraries.org/content/ebooks-and-DCL

15. Koerber, J. (2012). Espress yourself. *Library Journal, 137*(16), 23–26.

16. Carpenter, M., Graybill, J., Offord, J., & Piorun, M. (2011). Envisioning the library's role in scholarly communication in the year 2025. *Portal: Libraries & the Academy, 11*(2), 659–681.

17. Hahn, K. (2008). Research library publishing services: New options for university publishing. http://www.arl.org/bm~doc/research-library-publishing-services.pdf

18. Walters, T. (2012). The future role of publishing services in university libraries. *Portal: Libraries & the Academy, 12*(4), 425–454.

19. Nichols, D., Rowlands, I., Watkinson, A., Brown, D., & Jamali, H. (2012). Digital repositories ten years on: What do scientific researchers think of them and how do they use them? *Learned Publishing, 25*(3), 195–206.

20. Antelman, K. (2006). Self-archiving practice and the influence of publisher policies in the social sciences. *Learned Publishing, 19*(2), 85–95.

21. Bohlin, I. (2004). Communication regimes in competition: The current transition in scholarly communication seen through the lens of the sociology of technology. *Social Studies of Science, 34*(3), 365–391.

22. Covey, D. (2009). Self-archiving journal articles: A case study of faculty practice and missed opportunity. *Portal: Libraries & the Academy, 9*(2), 223–251.

23. Houghton, J. W. (2010). Economic implications of alternative publishing: Self-archiving and repositories. *Liber Quarterly, 19*(3/4), 275–292. The article also appears in *Prometheus, 28*(1), where many others discuss and critique Houghton's article extensively.

24. Harnad, S. (2008). Self-archiving, metrics, and mandates. *Science Editor, 31*(2), 57–59.

25. Nichols, D., Rowlands, I., Watkinson, A., Brown, D., & Jamali, H. (2012). Digital repositories ten years on: What do scientific researchers think of them and how do they use them? *Learned Publishing, 25*(3), 195–206.

Index